LOU REED
AND THE VELVET UNDERGROUND

By Diana Clapton

PROTEUS BOOKS LONDON & NEW YORK

PROTEUS BOOKS is an imprint of
The Proteus Publishing Group

United States
PROTEUS PUBLISHING CO., INC.
733 Third Avenue
New York, NY 10017
distributed by:
THE SCRIBNER BOOK COMPANIES, INC.
597 Fifth Avenue
New York, NY 10017

United Kingdom
PROTEUS (PUBLISHING) LIMITED
Bremar House,
Sale Place
London W2 1PT

ISBN 0 86276 0550 (paperback)
ISBN 0 86276 0569 (hardback)
First published in U.S. 1982
First published in U.K. 1982
Copyright © 1982

Design: Paul Stinson
Editor: Nicky Hodge
Typeset: SX Composing Ltd., Rayleigh, Essex
Printed by: Printer Industria Grafica sa, Barcelona, Spain
D.L.B. 29269 – 1982

LOU REED
AND THE VELVET UNDERGROUND

By Diana Clapton

Dedication:
This is for Bester, Father and Sainte-Blanche.

Thank you:

First, gratitude and affection to my editors, Nicky Hodge and Lucy McCullough, for their support. To Rusty Hamilton, Mikael Kirke and Fran Pelzman for research, suggestions and diplomacy. To Barbara Pepe, Maggie and Jeff Cason, without whose generosity and thoughtfulness this would be much worse. To Philip Milstein of the Velvet Underground Appreciation Society, and to Francesca Strauss, Johnathan Blank, Monty, Chopin and Phoebe the K, on Paws Control, the great Wolff, Mr. Vom, the beautiful Dennis Dedalus and, lastly, to John Morthland for heartsblood kindness when nothing else mattered.

July 1982

1. . . . AS A YOUNG APOSTATE
2. THE VELVET UNDERGROUND AND NICO
3. WHITE LIGHT/WHITE HEAT
4. THE VELVET UNDERGROUND
5. LOADED
6. THE VELVET UNDERGROUND LIVE AT MAX'S
7. LOU REED (SOLO)
8. TRANSFORMER
9. BERLIN
10. ROCK N ROLL ANIMAL AND 1969 VELVET UNDERGROUND LIVE
11. SALLY CAN'T DANCE AND LOU REED LIVE
12. METAL MACHINE MUSIC
13. CONEY ISLAND BABY
14. SHE'S MY BEST FRIEND
15. LIVE WITH CLIVE: THE ARISTA YEARS
16. GROWING UP IN PUBLIC
17. THE BLUE MASK
    DISCOGRAPHY

I am an inventor more deserving far than all those who have preceded me; a musician, moreover, who has discovered something like the key of love . . . I do not regret my old portion of divine gaiety: the sober air of this bleak countryside feeds vigorously my divine scepticism. But since this scepticism cannot, henceforth, be put to use, and since, moreover, I am dedicated to a new torment — I expect to become a very vicious madman.

Arthur Rimbaud, *Illuminations* **(1871)**

INTRODUCTION

In terms of rock & roll, Lou Reed is our finest failed priest. On his shoulders has fallen the burden of expressing the pain, hope, desperation and false promises of the last seventeen years of American life. He has approached our worst nightmares from the stance of pure poetry, adopting the role of the dramatic reader; a part of his message is that there is indeed the chance for redemption, but all the possibilities have to be considered.

In founding the Velvet Underground with John Cale, he offered faith as a form of musical expression, although it may not have seemed so at the time. Conceived in perfect freedom, the group violated the prime show biz raison d'être, which is that it was there to entertain. Where other bands offered escapism and good times, the Velvet Underground offered blunt confrontation, rhythmic despair, the realism of desperate choices, the smell of the dragon's tail rustling in the dry leaves, in a totally original musical form. Mostly, says Sterling Morrison, "People *hated* us."

Lou was a streetwise update of Kerouac's Dharma Bum; he too almost always found his "Boddhisatvas" in the street. In back-alley biblical terms he wrote about people, as Lester Bangs observed, "about whom nobody else gives a shit." He became their storyteller, to this day the best we have, an ascetic, moralistic voyeur/raconteur who explored life from the wild side, the underside, finding small answers. He always moved towards the white light, but his detours were confusing, and most of the time, you couldn't dance to 'em.

As to natural gifts, he is a sublime poet, as profound on the vagaries of human need as any world-class wordsmith he studied under Delmore Schwartz.

What John Rockwell terms his "limited, insecure baritone," serves him well as a medium of expression, focusing attention on the ageless power of his lyrics. The emotional evocation of what might be considered his four-album passion play, the four offerings of the Velvet Underground, continues to yield up meaning in an age where questions of faith have become bad jokes or simplistic cop-outs. Lou Reed will never let you off that easily.

Vulnerable, arrogant, dependent, great-looking, stoned, straight, glib, abusive and unutterably charming, he contained multitudes indeed, often four or five perfectly formed concepts at direct odds. On a personal level, in my interviewing experience, this was a man deeply and desperately loved even through his two specialties, the lapse of taste and the lawsuit. Hurtling through life with a real outlaw passion, genuinely regretting the lack of available risks, of darkened seas to sail, he almost became every sorry cliché in the rock mausoleum. Just *almost*. He seemed to realise instinctively that a wretchedly self-destructive death in Paris is only romantic to read about in bed. Image alteration was a primary source of amusement, but the real point was nothing less than personal salvation.

"Watch out, the world's behind you." . . . and finally caught up with him, not with censure or even a warrant for indecent exposure, but a hard-won comprehension few other artists would have the smarts to hope for. Finally his savage visions and wise-ass humor and searing tenderness make impeccable sense, as there are no easy escapes anymore. What was alien and terrifying becomes a natural part of daily city life. He will not play the guru and the shaman and offer gently symbolic solutions, but insist, instead, that we be absolutely aware, that we refuse the easy alternative of even the most stylish failure and loss.

...AS A YOUNG APOSTATE

Louis Alan Reed was born on March 2, 1942 into the upwardly mobile Brooklyn bourgeoisie, and soon began considering the alternatives. His parents were successful tax accountants who raised their sensitive, nervous first-born with considerable advantages. He started classical piano at age 8. In his early teens the family (now including a sister) moved to Freeport, Long Island. Lou attended public school, was bar mitvah'ed, and took up the guitar.

He played in school bands and cut his first record at the age of 14 – *So Blue*, with the Shades. It earned, according to a later interview in *People*, royalties of 78 cents. He announced his intentions of continuing with his musical career, which appalled his parents. They were also not thrilled with his taste for lowlife Long Island rock and roll bars. "I played in hoodlum bands where there were fights," he said in his first bio for RCA Records in 1972. In high school he went through a period of depression which alarmed his parents into making him go through electroshock therapy; the experience was so traumatizing that he turned it into a painful song over a decade later, *Kill Your Sons.* Though throughout his adolescence he grew away from his parents, he never totally separated himself from their influence, nor their middle-class materialism, nor even their protective, judgmental system of values.

In the early 60's, rich, young and snotty, he attended Syracuse University. He was well-read and wrote acceptable poetry, played guitar in a number of bands, including L.A. and the Eldorados and had already mastered a gangster/prankster sense of humor that would get him into a great deal of trouble.

At Syracuse he studied creative writing with the American poet Delmore Schwartz. A large, compulsive man, Schwartz never learned to master "the scrimmage of appetite" within himself. The phrase is from his poem, *The Heavy Bear:* "The hungry beating brutish one/ In love with candy, anger and sleep". Schwartz lectured on Eliot, Joyce, Rilke and Yeats. "He was the first great man that I had ever met," Lou would sing on an album dedicated to him much later. A raging romantic with a dazzling, uneven reputation, declamatory gifts, a string of beautiful young women to do things like bail him out of jail, and a god-awful booze/ benzedrine habit, he became Lou's lifelong role model. There was one crucial difference: Lou may have learnt to understand the Latin puns in *Finnegan's Wake,* but he was, at bedrock, a good Jewish boy from Long Island, a survivor.

Below Lou in the dormitory lived a lanky, insolent guitarist named Sterling Morrison. Sterling knew he had a soulmate nearby when he heard Lou fire up his own Stratocaster "to disturb the R.O.T.C. – they'd drill right behind the dormitory. The moment they hit the field he'd crank up very loud. Or else play bagpipe music – he was great fun." Lou also operated as a D-J for the college radio station, and often came to pilfer Sterling's records: "What we really had in common was we both liked black music." They also shared foul, formative nights in Long Island bar bands and an identical sense of style. "I was," Sterling remembers with some pride, "inspired by delinquency. It was fun to be smart, but it was much better to . . . package it as a delinquent."

Sterling began his academic career at the University of Illinois, where he was an Engineering Physics major. Requested to take his cavalier attitude elsewhere by the Dean of Men ("Boy, was he hot – I'd simply refused to attend class") he brought his now-unusable Regents Scholarship to Syracuse, where he investigated the sciences and then moved on to English Literature. "Lou and I both did very well. But Lou was in deep trouble by senior year. Supposedly he was thrown out of school for drug abuse – no. The hottest hot water he got into

Kees Tabak, Retna Ltd

was political. There was a quarterly poetry magazine that he contributed to – along with Carl Stoker, Lincoln Swadoes and Jim Tucker (brother of Maureen). It was quite well received, as the first issue so, when everyone else crapped out, Lou took it upon himself to get out issue #2. But he decided to include a diatribe against the student head of the Young Americans for Freedom – I guess the thing was in real bad taste. The father of this student was a very powerful corporation lawyer and decided this was libelous, and he'd bust Lou's ass. So they hauled him before the Dean – but this guy and his father were so offensive, the Dean started to shift to Lou's side. Afterwards the Dean told him to finish up his work and get his ass out of there, and nothing would happen to him . . .''

inherent injustice of being both a Jew and a genius at Harvard University. The poet, idolized by his students, peers and a world-wide cult of admirers since *In Dreams Begin Responsibilities*, was dying of drug and alcohol abuse, a splendid sun going down. During one of his harangues, he announced to Lou that he, too, was truly a poet, and that if he ever "sold out" he, Delmore, would come after him. Fifteen years later Lou remembered the influence with considerable warmth in *Rolling Stone:* "It must have been really incredible to have been goodlooking, a poet and be straight."

But artist and acolyte never made it together past the campus walls. When Delmore came to live in Greenwich Village, paranoid and overwrought, he refused to see Lou, or even answer his letters (or anyone else's).

Lou, not yet a "heavy bear", perhaps never to become one, was instead a brilliant, vulnerable and very adventurous honey-bear. He had Schwartz's rage to live and cool, cerebral gift for literary analysis. When one almost-adolescent could combine an overt scag habit with the ability to incorporate Joyce's passion for linguistic precision and use of symbolism to heighten mood, he was certainly on his way to a future in the poetry biz. There were risks. His teacher would soon die, solitary and suspicious, in a squalid cubicle of the Chelsea Hotel.

Lou had to consider all the options. In the book *Nobody Waved Goodbye,* he wrote, "I had recently been introduced to drugs by a mashed-in-faced Negro . . . named Jaw. Jaw gave me hepatitis immediately, which is pathetic and laughable at once." He could not share his classmates' love of the "innocent" Beatles; "I, after all, had had jaundice."

At college he was also very tight with Jim Tucker, fellow English major, rock rat and tom-fooler. Jim had a younger sister named Maureen who had also just been awarded a Regents' Scholarship, which she was planning on using at Nassau Community College. Maureen spent a lot of time listening to records by the African drummer Olatunji. Like Sterling, who was a trumpet prodigy before he picked up a guitar, Maureen studied the clarinet for four years to prepare for becoming a guitarist and then moving on to drums.

While Lou was running amok during his senior year, Maureen — Moe — was attending college and drumming in an all-boy band from Levittown. "It was Olatunji, finally, who de-

Even Sterling admits that "Lou was being pretty sleazy. Syracuse was a private school, and actually very tolerant, but I guess they'd seen a few too many spectacles at the Orange Bar at his hands . . . and mine." There were lots of drugs. Lou would be on the unmistakable nod outside and inside the Orange, as Delmore Schwartz, his "spiritual godfather", was roaring away about Eliot's love life and the

cided me on drums. With the guitar I could play chords but never, really, lead. As a surprise, my mother bought this $50, fourth-hand drum set with one cymbal — it looked like a beat-up hubcap. A bass drum and a snare and that was it. I started bangin' away and after five minutes I said, Okay, this is what I want. I guess rhythm was always the most important part of music to me."

Whisked out of his college town by authoritarian forces for "various clandestine operations I was alleged to have been involved in," the young Louis breezed back to his home turf and entered his pop-protest period. He started writing songs for a do-it-yourself record company named Pickwick Studios, which turned out el cheapo singles and albums called Supermarket Specials. As a staff writer, Lou wrote, sang and played guitar for such gems as *Cycle Annie, You're Driving Me Insane* and *The Ostrich*, which included its own absolutely original dance style: "You put your head on the floor and have someone step on it." Pickwick Studios thought this was wonderful and wanted to put together a band to go out and promote the thing. This was never actualized, and head stomping did not become fashionable until Black Sabbath was invented.

"We happened upon the scene about the time Lou was phasing out," says Sterling. "We thought maybe we'd all get in on it — but there was no money coming out. So we were just . . . lurking around. The Beechnuts and the Roughnecks — Lou and God knows who, not real bands."

Just before the artist sang his last Supermarket Special he met John Cale. Cale was a Welsh viola and piano prodigy, a classically-trained singer and composer of swashbuckling beauty. Lou and Sterling were bowled over. "He was incredible — started piano at 3, viola at 5, then gave his first BBC performance when he was 8 — a true phenomenon!" Almost twenty years later, Sterling Morrison is still awed. John went on to Goldsmiths College in South London and the Royal Academy of Music, where he dazzled his peers and corresponded with John Cage. "But even when he was at the Royal Academy he was beyond the avant-garde — beyond the pale. He rebelled totally against his classical training. But Lou and I felt we could make use of it somehow . . ."

John, who shared a respect for right order that matched Lou's and Sterling's, had recently outraged the Tanglewood Summer Festival by destroying a table with an axe during an avant-garde presentation. In New York he was working with LaMonte Young's Dream Syndicate, exploring extended electronic drones and eerie, ethereal subconscious musical forms that baffled easy analysis.

The three fell into a deep, intense, intimate friendship that all still speak of as love — and why not? They were each brilliant, gorgeous, freewheeling, arch-romantics with musical gifts. They had the world by the short hairs, and they mostly liked the same drugs, which included Valium, Thorazine, amphetamine and booze. In the evenings they went to parties.

Lou was eager to impress John with his songs. He had already written the apocalyptic *Heroin* and *Waiting for the Man* while serving up the shlock at Pickwick, but his employers were not interested in songs about copping and mainlining that 8th Graders couldn't dance to. John was not interested either. "Most of the music written then was like folk — and he played his songs with an acoustic guitar," he told Mary Harron in *Punk*. "I couldn't give a shit about folk music. But he kept shoving these lyrics in front of me. They were very different, very literate, and he was writing about things other people weren't."

The three formed a band called the Primitives, with Scots poet and mystic Angus MacLise on drums. Having studied drone music in India, and also influenced by other dreamlike Eastern forms, Angus had "radically different ideas about rhythm and percussion," according to Sterling. 'Not 2/4 or 4/4 drumming, but something more . . . off-beat. And drones . . . reinforced the viola." They played around New York at various parties and happenings. In those days good music was pouring out of every café door in the East and West Village, and there was precious little "high seriousness" (one of Sterling's least favourite terms) about performance.

The Primitives progressed, as did their recreational tastes, to the Falling Spikes. Angus' mystical roots were becoming disturbed . . . the loud, abrasive, band ("I figured one way of getting on everyone's nerves was to have improvisation going on for any length of time," said John) actually had fans. In his heart Angus knew that art and capitalism — being paid in any way to play — should never mix. "He sincerely believed that if you were making money you should be doing something other than what you wanted to," explains Sterling. "He was really out there . . . this really bothered him."

11

THE VELVET UNDERGROUND AND NICO

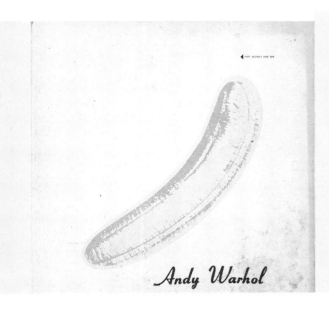

Andy Warhol

Danny Fields: *Why did people seem more fabulous then?*

Lou: *. . . There were all these people who were fabulous. And one of the reasons they were fabulous is that they were in public, and you had access to all these incredible people. And now you don't.*

Danny: *Do you regret the passing of that?*

Lou: *Yes and no. I don't think I could take it again.*

The most powerfully innovative, enduringly influential and organically self-destructive musical group of its time was founded one day in 1965 when Angus MacLise picked up a porno paperback called *The Velvet Underground*. It cost 60 cents, was written by Michael Leigh, and promised the lowdown on "the sexual corruption of our age". The band, then playing the sado-masochistic masterpiece, *Venus in Furs* to aroused amazement in lower Manhattan, found the linkup too good to pass up: "Okay, we're the Velvet Underground."

Here was a band conceived in perfect freedom. Questioned on what motivated him towards remunerative musical employment,

Sterling Morrison said, "Professional career? I didn't think we could make *records*. Music was what we did for fun — and any time I found an opportunity to have fun, I would seize it." Lou was similarly cavalier: "We had no ambition at all. We were underground people and, basically, we were into the scene . . . People were into a lot of different things," he told Dave Hickey in *Oui*, "like make-up, and doing a lot of amphetamines."

Post writer Al Aronowitz secured the band's first gig, opening for the Myddle Class at a high school dance in Summit, New Jersey. They would be paid the fee of $75 — Angus freaked. He just knew it would come to this — a lifetime of good karma down the drain. He noted, with alarm, that they'd already had something approximating to a "publicity photo" taken by Lou's neighbor in Freeport. Guilt-ridden visions of becoming an early Led Zep ran through his brain. Angus quit cold.

Their very first paid booking was approaching, and they grasped desperately for another drummer. "At that point, I was the only one they could grab — the only one with a drum kit," recalls Moe Tucker. Barely twenty, she was hurtled into the big time in the gym of the Summit High School. Raw sex in jeans, studs and black leather, they played *There She Goes Again, Venus in Furs* and *Heroin*. Two girls fainted. There were no encores.

Art as antagonism — didn't Rimbaud start out like this? The songs were powerful, even malevolent — with Lou's howling "ostrich guitar" and John's bloodcurdling viola, which he used as a sumurai with a favourite saber, they became almost an act of war. In the East Village this was considered reasonable late evening entertainment. In the provinces — boding ill for cross-country tours — the Velvet Underground violated all existing community standards.

Moe, though, would stay. A friend of Sterling's for ten years, she knew she would be an anomaly. Straight and sane, she chose to dive into what Patti Smith would later term "the sea of possibility". "When I started, there weren't any women playing *any* instruments in rock and roll bands, let alone 'men's' instruments. But it worked. It was weird — I wound up having a close relationship with each member of the group. Because they're certainly not the type of people I'd choose as friends . . ."

She was up for anything. "We'd gotten very used to Angus' offbeat drumming," says Sterling, "so we had Moe play standing up — that

would make it more difficult for her to get back in the old patterns." Fine. Through every performance she watched Lou worshipfully and wide-eyed, waiting for cues.

Their next paid performance was at the Café Bizarre, a tourist trap with a hawker, on MacDougal Street. Lou played rhythm and "ostrich", a rewiring that enabled his instrument to project multiple tones for every string plucked, Sterling lead, Cale alternating on bass and viola, and Moe pounding out a heavy, hypnotic, martial beat. They were incredibly loud. John was "becoming very constructive in my use of the viola," refining and redefining the mysteries of distortion. They looked marvellous, like passionate pirates on a summer outing, but their music was a menace. It was like a fireball, spreading out into a silent audience of baffled suburbanites, engulfing them. All the audience wanted was to play bohemians for the night! After about a week the manager told them that if they let loose their sonic barrage again entitled *The Black Angel's Death Song,* it was curtains. Ever faithful to their state-of-the-art arrogance, they started the very next set with it.

"And I swear," remembers Sterling, "that was the very best it was ever played." *The Black Angel's Death Song* is a masterpiece, a consistent critic's choice. It begins on a note of repressed hysteria and continues with rising desperation to a hideous climax of atonal feedback. Lou mutters some existential prattle, about epiphany's terror hurling us into the arms of the cosy brown snow of the east; on first hearing it makes the blood run cold.

Those present, most emphatically the manager, felt otherwise, and the group soon found themselves back on the sidewalk. By chance, during that week, Gerard Malanga, poet and filmmaker whose fancy it was at the time to sit on the right hand of Andy Warhol, had wandered in. Entranced, he had dragged Warhol down to the club . . . and the media master concurred. At this point, this provocative American artist, whose creations, happenings, philosophy and above all, lifestyle, had catapulted him to the heights of hip chic, was fascinated with sensual assault. Warhol's whole artistic life was a projector, throwing off vivid images on any flat surface. For years he and Gerard, whose looks were those of a fine piece of Italian sculpture, strode about in black leather, visually flirting with S/M images . . . disturbing right order.

Warhol was enchanted with the Velvets, as

they were immediately termed by the cognoscenti. Why? Because, as he wrote in his literary lowdown of the 60's, *Popism,* "People would leave (the café) looking dazed and damaged." This was the audience response to be desired . . . mere approbation was so damn trite. His instincts told him he had found a rock group that could become even more threatening, assaultive . . . artistically correct. "And Andy," said Sterling — and, at one time or another, every member of the band, "was never wrong."

Warhol was approaching the height of his powers, and booked on an ever-widening lecture circuit to explain his art, philosophy and films. He needed a musical medium of expression. Donovan, the Byrds, and the Washington Square folkies with their dirty feet did not engage him. His films dealt with the same subjects as those Lou Reed had forged into empassioned poetry . . . desperation, drugs, beauty, dreams, rage, escape and pan-sexual perversity. An instant sympathy sprang up between the two forcefields. "He became our . . . catalyst," said John Cale later. "Whoever he works with, he takes and sets off very well."

The Velvets first Warhol gig was a stunner. They appeared at a benefit week at the Cinemateque, in aid of the underground filmmakers. "We did the Andy Warhol Uptight for free . . . and made them $13,000," recalls Sterling. Their impact was considerable. Even though the largely artsy, funky crowd was ready for anything, lured to the flickering lights by scenemakers Barbara Rubin and Robby Neuwirth, the hysterical viola drone during *Heroin* knocked 'em out. "We left *bodies* behind," remembers Sterling, with glee. Everyone was ecstatic.

Here began the hysterical, halcyon days of the earliest and greatest years of the Velvet Underground. These luminous times, which have glowed in rock history as perhaps the most savage, stylish and splendid, were centered on the Factory, Warhol's legendary working – and playing – loft. It was at 231 East 47th Street, one floor down from the roof. Billy Linich, the resident concierge, lighting genius and mystic, covered the whole thing in aluminum foil. Here the Velvets hung out, and worked out new songs. They were surrounded by a grotesque assortment of beautiful people on drugs, which were amusing in those days. Aspiring starlets, gorgeous hustlers, malleable heiresses – Edie Sedgwick was the most flamboyant – trust-fund trendies, film freaks, amphetamine misfits, gallery owners, drug and art groupies, society matrons who had found illumination through Factory "fun times", and hunky or handy delivery boys: they had one prevailing ethic, and that was to escape the normalcy of the late 60's, the means, while amusing, being much less important than the end.

Witty and urbane Danny Fields, who had fled medical school for the incandescence of Factory life, remembers meeting Lou. "I first heard *Heroin* and I thought it was beautiful music. But I was terrified of Lou. I was always trying to figure out things to say to him that would be cool — because he was so cool and sharp. *Everybody* was in love with him back then. Around 1965, he was the sexiest boy in town. He still is." Danny quickly became the Evelyn Waugh of downtown chic. Where our nation has perhaps lost a combination surgeon/stand-up comedian, we have gained the 60's most astute oral historian. Lou looked "good

and pubescent" then, observed Warhol, and the two forged a productive, supportive friendship that has endured. In each of his books, Warhol pays tribute to Lou, delighted by his radical capacity to change, endure, risk everything and survive. They seemed to share a common attitude towards experience — that it must be enjoyed, even wallowed in (although neither fit the libertine label) but above all, made productive.

Danny's apartment was the beachhead for the onslaught of the "Cambridge kids" or the "young Jewish set", mostly wealthy and playful girls and boys, of which the young, high-strung and uninhibited Edie was the centre jewel. The privilege of being near Andy Warhol was considered the triumph of their lives. Bedazzled, many ephemera strayed too close to the light. In the midst of all the ego collisions and nudity, screaming guitars and parties, Danny remembers observing, "We all had this feeling about Lou — that he would bury us. He was much too

The Velvet Underground — Sterling Morrison, Lou Reed, John Cale and Angus MacLise

smart to get sucked into the whirlpool. Others may have been too fragile, too beautiful to survive – but he knew what he was doing."

"It really wasn't that decadent, or unsavory, a scene as the press has made it," contends Sterling. "Supposedly there was an orgy every two hours. Oh, these things did happen – there was a lot of foolishness – but the attitude towards sex was blasé. It wasn't naughty. It wasn't even remarkable. Whatever people did in the back rooms at parties, or in the bathrooms, just happened. We had a great, great time. There were parties every single night. That was one of the day's big decisions . . . to figure out where you were going to eat, and then what parties to grace. You could just drift. There was always enough money."

Even tomboy Maureen felt comfortable there. "I never got left behind. Sometimes I'd just go up to the Factory and hang around, for fun. I liked those people. You'd be surprised – they could be very considerate. As I was the only girl in the band, even Gerard and Andy watched out for me."

There were lots of drugs, mainly speed and acid. Who did how much of what is not clear, although it's a cinch no member of the Velvet Underground sat around sipping Kool-Aid and re-working *There She Goes Again.* Speed led to nattering, babbling, fussy behavior, impotence and attention to detail. Lou played the voyeur/raconteur to the hilt. Through the madness, Lou especially, distorted his responses only to the point where they amused him, never fully losing control. He enjoyed the imbalances, the fallout, the idea that every moment was self-inventing. Someday he'd turn it into incredible songs.

Into this splendour came the moon-goddess Nico. Nico was a German fashion model in her mid-twenties from a small farm village south of Berlin; her blonde beauty was so magnificent that, by all accounts, to meet her was to fall in love. She had a low, mellow voice, with the timbre of a fine cello, and she spoke — whispered — a broken English that seemed the language of dreams. Delivered to the Factory by the equally extra-terrestrial Brian Jones, her aura of enchantment stopped all the craziness in its tracks. She pulled a single from her handbag that, she murmured, "Bawwb Dee-lahnn" had written for her. Further investigation revealed she had already had an interesting single produced in England by Jimmy Page. She had also had a child, Ari, by French matinee wowser Alain Delon. And not only that; she had played a stunning bit part in Fellini's *La Dolce Vita.*

Even the pragmatist Warhol saw her as the perfect lead singer for the Velvets — and Lou, so bedazzled he momentarily forgot that that was his job, agreed. "How could we *dislike* the idea?" felt Sterling — at first. Realising that her mournful tones, like extended sobs, did not lend themselves to the electric rage of *The Black Angel's Death Song,* Lou wrote three new pieces. *All Tomorrow's Parties, Femme Fatale* and *I'll Be Your Mirror* were about Nico — and Nico's observations of other women around the Factory, not that many of whom were thrilled with her. Moe, who was and is very well-balanced, felt "she was a shmuck, from the first. She was this beautiful person who had travelled through Europe being a semi-star. Her ego had grown very large. Don't get me wrong; the songs Lou wrote for her were great, and she did them very well. Her accent made them great, but there was a limit!"

All five moved on to the Exploding Plastic Inevitable, Warhol's multi-media assault,

which radicalized the New York music scene. Its beauty, savagery and talent has never been matched by even the light/laser shows of Heavy Metal. The grand opening was in the early spring of 1966 at the Dom, the old Polish National Social Hall, on St. Mark's Place. It looked like the foyer of hell — well documented by the back cover photo on the first album. In musical and visual ferocity it was an update of the Götterdämmerung, complete with warriors and Valkyries dancing in derangement on and off stage.

The Velvets were centre stage, with Gerard Malanga in black leather performing his reptilian, mesmerizing whip dance. Ingrid Superstar or Mary Waronov, in splendid disarray, writhed nearby. All around the room Warhol's films, as "Vinyl", were projected, while the coloured lights of the images fell over the band. The experience was like an acid trip, a hallucination with the power of a dream. The blue light played over Nico's shimmering blonde hair, and Cale's viola was all but an aural mugging.

Warhol was right: entertainment as assault had a future. His genuine imprimatur was a lure. Fans drove in from faraway Long Island night after night. Yet the band which was playing the music it wanted to hear, never considered becoming popular. "We just had fun," recalls Sterling. "It was such a wild scene. Nico did her songs — but when she wasn't singing, really, we had nothing else for her to do. She wasn't that integral a part of the band." This was lost on many, if not all, onlookers. "Nico is standardly more than standardly beautiful visually," wrote Richard Meltzer in *The Aesthetics of Rock,* "so it wouldn't matter whether or not she could sing." Sensing this, says Sterling, "she was always pushing to sing more songs, and we kept resisting." "I kept to myself," recalls Moe, "until she wanted to sing *Heroin.* But then I *had* to speak my piece."

Moe was also not impressed by Nico's sexual politics. "When she felt Lou had all the power, she went with him. And then, when John had more influence. . . . That stuff made me have no respect for her at all."

Nico's preferences mostly ran to young, beautiful boys. The winner was the 16-year-old Jackson Browne, a doe-eyed dreamer who wrote three songs for her and followed her everywhere. "Oh I just can't believe it!" he confided to Richard Meltzer, who did not share his swoon, "a mere teenager in from sunny California for less than a month and I'm sleep-

20

ing with *the most* beautiful girl in the world!"

Warhol and the group took a three-year lease on the hall. "But through politics and corruption, our lease was waived," says Sterling. "Albert Grossman planted one of his stooges in the box office – and it was his idea that we then do a West Coast tour. When we came back in May, they had seized the building and re-named it The Balloon Farm, and we were out. Oh, we could play there and be paid a few hundred a night – but we found the idea repellent. That was the beginning of all our trouble in New York."

The first Velvet Underground West Coast tour was a combination nightmare and laff-riot, like many of their gigs. Warhol had decided to fianance an actual album, and called in his friend Tom Wilson to help produce part of it. The brilliant classic instantly legendary *Banana* album, which "was recorded, basically in eight hours," says Moe. "We pooled our money with Andy, and could afford only eight hours of studio time in New York. Tom Wilson produced only one of the songs, *Sunday Morning*. Then, when we hit the West Coast, MGM who had signed us because of the Warhol connection gave us three more hours at TTG Studios to clean things up. I think we did *Heroin* over and repaired the vocals on *Waiting for the Man*."

Tinseltown was agog at the Exploding Plastic Inevitable's assault on their jaded senses. The group was booked at the Trip, yet audience reaction was mixed. After one performance Cher, flouncing out, remarked that, "It will replace nothing – except maybe suicide." Andy was delighted, and included the comment in their publicity. Leather lovely and film fiend Jim Morrison was also in the audience, though, and he was very impressed.

The sheriff's office closed down the club after a week. The band was advised to hang out to collect the money contractually owed. They lived at the Castle, a huge, stone, medieval building up in the hills by the Mt. Wilson Observatory. They had nothing to do but get into trouble. Fans delivered all sorts of amusements. "Things got very hazy," Cale later told Robert Greenfield, "and Severn Darden brought this young chick up to meet me . . . after five nights at the Castle, I don't think I even got her address." Nico retreated into her waking dream state, stalking the grounds in majesty trailed by sycophants.

Bill Graham called and demanded they play the Fillmore (in San Francisco), home turf of the

Airplane, the Dead and other brotherly love bands. They knew this was a mistake. While Sterling flew back to City College to take his final exams the rest, against their better judgment, went north. Sterling flew in directly from his finals. "I knew there was trouble – I was thrown out of the club the moment I arrived. The rest of the band was at some swell cocktail party, and apparently Graham was annoyed that he hadn't been invited. Plus he'd already had some words with Andy and Paul Morrissey. Graham came in our dressing room opening night and hissed, 'I hope you mothers bomb.' We looked at him in disbelief.

"We didn't bomb. We set the attendance record and revealed the Fillmore to the whole Berkeley contingent. But he still hated us. One time on stage there was some lunacy, and Lou was thrashing the cymbals with his guitar. The hi-hat was rocking back and forth and finally just rocked off the back drum platform. It hit Lou in the head and gave him a real scalp cut. He was bleeding a lot – but the show must go on! Meanwhile Graham, so sympathetic, is in the wings, screaming, 'I got no insurance! I got no insurance!'

"So when we left the stage, we just leaned our guitars up against the amplifiers and strolled off. They all started to feed back – great noise! They had to cut the power for the whole place to shut down the noise onstage. We were furious by the end, but our road manager reminded us not to get rambunctious, because we were paid by cheque. But if I ever run into him again . . ."

On the return trip they played Chicago but Lou had to check into a hospital with hepatitis. Sterling and John sent for Angus immediately. "Nico was in Europe making commercials and Andy was somewhere else – we were essentially thrown to the wolves. But it didn't work out exactly like that. They held us over a week.

"Angus found out it wasn't the way he envisioned. We gave him a sackful of money and told him he could stay anywhere in the city. He wandered all around, out to the Bahai temple, and had a wonderful time. John and I rearranged all the songs. It was the most organized rehearsal time in the entire history of the Velvet Underground. We put Angus on drums, moved Moe over to rhythm and bass – on which she was more than capable – John did fulltime keyboards and I played guitar. John sang all the leads. It was remarkable – we were *good*.

"Lou got progressively more paranoid, back

in the hospital, as the good reports filtered back. At that point I realised the permanent change I really wanted in the band. I thought it would be a tremendous advantage to somehow find a permanent bass player and have John play nothing but viola and keyboards. Lou did not approve of this – possibly because, with Nico, this would've made six on stage. Or cheapness, or ego . . . anyway, it never happened.

"Angus was still running on his own time. For one performance, he showed up twenty minutes late. After the whole thing he kept flailing away for twenty minutes to make up for the time lost. We were down in the bar drinking and he was up there thrashing away at these odd percussion instruments. People left looking dazed.

"Even at this point we'd almost completely worked out *Sister Ray*, as an instrumental. We were continually refining. I still think our best performances were never recorded."

Lou recovered with his usual resilience and they made it back to New York, where, says Sterling, "everyone had heard good stories and was very enthusiastic." But this was the beginning of the end of their local popularity, starting with the hassles at the newly-named Balloon Farm. They played two gigs there then Andy found space uptown at the Gymnasium, but "we couldn't get the lease to the building. In those days bands rented a place and stayed. The Mothers of Invention took a hall in the Village and played every night for two years. They were strictly a money-making proposition," says Sterling. "But I had *other* ideas." The Velvets played at Stavros Niarchos' wedding as Warhol's chic cachet counted most with those who could afford it . . . and at an event in Lincoln Center.

Meantime, the album for which Andy designed the special peel-off banana kept getting "lost". "There was such anarchy within our organization that we were sort of 'self-managed' – which meant everyone was manager for a day. Once in awhile, we'd show up at MGM to find out why things weren't progressing. But the manager for the Mothers of Invention was up there every single day, negotiating for his band. He *lived* up there. We had no idea what was going on . . . until later.

"The album was signed, sealed and delivered. We had our pictures and the cover design from Andy, and it was outstanding. But what do you know, the Mothers of Invention album came out first! Not only that, but the

2nd from left to right – Sterling, Nico, Cale, Lou and Betsey Johnson *Betsey Johnson*

manager got all the promotional support out of MGM . . . record displays in stores and radio support and so on. What we got was mostly banned.''

''We're already past the acid tripper stage,'' Lou had written in *Aspen Magazine*, but you couldn't prove it by a Mothers fan. They were The Competition, off-the-wall, iconoclastic, strange looking, drug-loving and loud. Maybe MGM thought there wasn't room for two wild and crazy bands, partly produced by Tom Wilson, in American musical tastes. They should have asked Lou: ''The freaks are winning, there's no doubt about it, everyone better empty their pockets.''

The Mothers had calculated their audience and how to empty its pockets. ''We never sat back,'' says Sterling, ''and figured, 'Gosh! Wonder what the kids would like to hear?' We never gave a shit. We just had this . . . very good record. Let's face it, it was not a serious, commercial pop music venture. My attitude was that I wanted to make the best rock and roll record with the songs I liked best — and here it is.''

Ah, the beleaguered *Banana* album. It could not be played on the radio because the lyrics were considered obscene. It could not even be advertised. MGM, deciding its Warhol connections would be sufficient hype, threw no support behind it. ''In a way it was suicide to release it. It had its own bad reviews — self-contained — on the inner cover. For a bit WBAI did play it, but then we had an argument with Bob Fass, so *he* wouldn't give it airplay. We couldn't get support and we couldn't get a place to play.

''I never did see my time with the Velvet Underground as a series of Great Moments in History, as far too many rock critics do. I did believe absolutely in what we were doing and the way we did it. We were well thought of in certain circles, and that was enough. But in commercial terms, we thought, 'This sort of thing hasn't been tried — let's just see what happens . . .' What happens is you get banned from the radio.''

The magnificent album staggered up to # 171 on the Billboard chart despite all. Symbolistic, visionary, perverse and haunting, it was certainly no match for *Sergeant Pepper*, released around that time, but certain critics gave it instant huzzahs and indeed supported the band from then on. In *Melody Maker*, Richard Williams termed it ''a scary document'' by a group with ''surrealistic charisma; the

John Cale *Chester Simpson*

music isn't cluttered up with pat, meaningless clichés.'' Other critics found it honest and urban, but were cautious about embracing even a masterwork full of whips, syringes and something entitled *The Black Angel's Death Song.* Most came around after about two years and now claim to have seen them as the definitive poetry-fired garage band from the very first.

''The *Banana* album went gold,'' says Sterling,'' but of course they never gave us one. The total sales were quite appreciable, even after MGM pulled it off the market because of

the Eric Emerson lawsuit. The original cover had a photo on the back, upside down, of Eric Emerson. When Eric got busted for acid and needed money for legal defence, he hit upon the idea of suing MGM. The truth was that it was a photo taken by Stephen Shore, used in a montage photographed by Hugo, who sold it to Andy, who sold it to MGM. So if anyone was going to get sued – it would have to go all the way back to Stephen Shore. But MGM panicked and pulled the thing off the market. We were furious! The photo was blacked out with a sticker, and then eventually it was airbrushed out. Eric had no legal grounds at all.''

Frustrated by events they could not control in New York, the Velvet Underground ''wanted to punish the city'' and decamped for Boston, where they were hotly appreciated and no critics wrote things like, ''the music alternates between cacaphony and the hideous 'acid' maundering of the (band's) insufferable, navel-gazing guitars,'' as Stephen Koch snapped in the otherwise acceptable *Stargazer*.

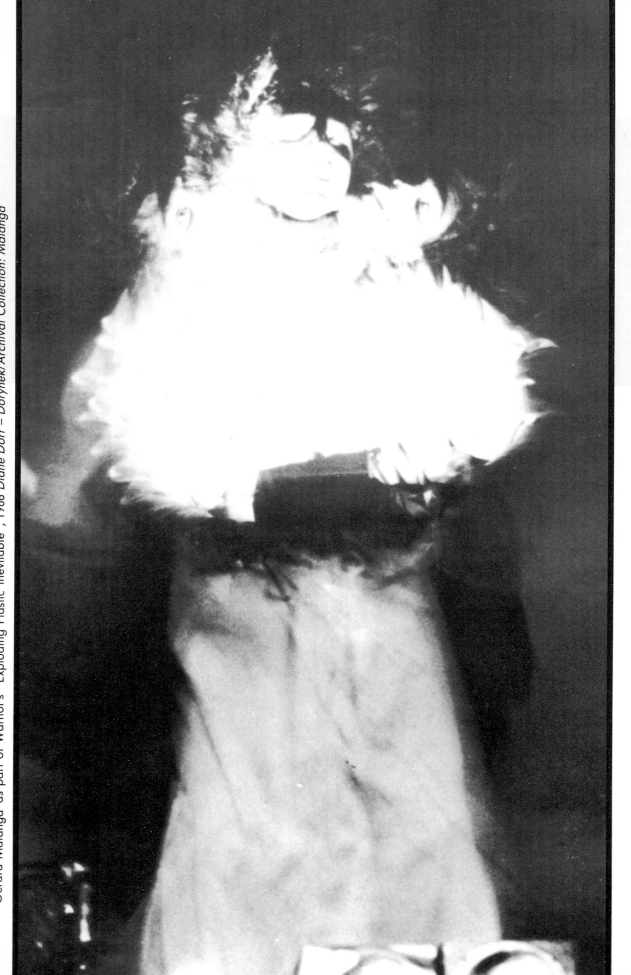

WHITE LIGHT/WHITE HEAT

WHITE LIGHT/WHITE HEAT
THE VELVET UNDERGROUND

MGM

Lou had worked for his father's accounting firm, so he had a strong background in the business side of things, and his feet never left the ground. Mine definitely did."
John Cale to Amos Poe in New York Rocker

With the approach of genuine publicity, egos began colliding. Lou began to grow into the part of the junkie desperado that a large part of his audience saw as the real person behind *Heroin.* "People assume," he mused in *Rolling Stone* eleven years later, "that what's on a record applies to the person singing it, and they find that shocking." The Warhol divine-decadence blessing gave them much of their clout. Too much, felt Cale. "That made us nervous — we really wanted to make it as a band."

White Light/White Heat, the second album, is the most manic, abrasive and powerful artifact of the Velvet Underground. It reflected the internal tensions of a band ascending into prominence and "at each others' throats", as Cale says. The desperate feedback and distortion gives an immediacy to the music that sounds like a backstage brawl. The intelligence in this scholastically accredited band could not offset the daily antagonisms of differing musical ideas. Some observers insist that Lou, at this point, realised he wanted to make it as a solo performer, regarding a band as a necessary but supportive evil.

John had produced, arranged and played on Nico's first solo album, *Chelsea Girl,* a magical piece containing three songs by Jackson Browne, with others by Dylan, Cale, Reed and Morrison. It too was under the Warhol aegis. Gentle, personal and loving, it was the direct antithesis of *White Light/White Heat,* though it also had depressive moments.

The creation of the *White Light/White Heat* album witnessed the best arguments of the band's history, as well as the violent departures of some members. No one ever did anything in cold, or even lukewarm, blood, except possibly Moe, and she commented: "The real reason I lasted was because I was the chick who didn't have ego problems."

At first, according to Sterling, ego wars washed over him. "We had plenty of opportunity on stage to do whatever we wanted. We could croak our harmonies any way we pleased. John and I did a lot of backup vocals — that was a riot in itself. Starting the song *White Light,* we'd sing together. One night John just kept silent, leaving me to squawk the lyrics. I thought, 'All right, I'll fix that son of a bitch.' The next time we did the song, I kept my mouth shut. This kind of stunt went on all the time. The audience would say, 'What the *hell* . . .?'

"John and I were close friends. We had lived together on Ludlow Street and 3rd Street — Lou didn't really live with us, he was around a lot. But our music did evolve collectively. Lou would walk in with some sort of scratchy verse and we would all develop the music . . . it almost always worked like that. We'd all thrash it out into something very strong. He never sat down and played songs for us to 'learn'. He could improvise very fast . . . just conjure up a lyric as we were playing. Then the songs would begin a whole new life in performance. I never felt that the value of the songs ever transcended their performance.

"My favourite song in performance was whichever one came across better than I anticipated. I always loved *Venus in Furs.* Usually I have a fondness for the first song on stage. For a long time we generally started out with *There She Goes Again,* which was getting progressively shorter and more off-the-wall. Some of my foibles were reflected in our song order, which it was my responsibility to set.

"And also, during this period, our image wasn't so perverse. We all had really good clothes in our photos. Betsey Johnson was designing clothes for us. She was great . . . we looked *good.* I personally wore the first tie-dyed shirt I'd ever seen. Betsey bought it on the street. She came with us the first time we played the Boston Tea Party, in 1967. The others she gave undershirts and said, 'Here!' Wear these.' But I get this wonderful shirt. Then I started sweating profusely and all the dye ran off onto my skin. The effect was like a monster film — horrific. It took about three weeks for me to wash it off. But she was designing suits and all kinds of outfits for us, really fine stuff.

"To my mind, the only thing that bothered me was equipment trouble. If my amp acted up, that pulled the rug out from under me. Usually things worked out — we'd rent from Chip Monck and others. But once when we played the Rhode Island School of Design, where they were very eager for us, we were stiffed — we had *no* sound. So we did all our songs without the vocals. That upset me a whole lot. Those people were really fans."

In autumn of '67 the album was recorded in a single day. "It was a quickie," recalls Moe, "because they never gave us much time. It was a very fast process with Tom Wilson in New York."

John recalls that as an unhappy time. "Lou and I couldn't see eye to eye anymore. We weren't rehearsing, we weren't working, we were flying all over the place and we couldn't concentrate on anything long enough to work. It was the result of touring day in and day out — which can be a detrimental influence," he told Michael Zilkha in *Interview*. In terms of emotional balance, he said in another interview, "there was no more room in the band for anyone else — Lou and I did enough fighting for all. We weren't very compatible writing together, but we did turn out a number of songs." Sterling, who dislikes strife, felt that John represented his own point of view in most disputes, "but I'd occasionally throw my weight in. Sometimes, though, I'd physically remove myself."

Even with the squabbling, a great deal of which was induced, many people felt, by John's staggering good looks and onstage flamboyance, the band had some good times together. The best, recalled Sterling, was at Philip Johnson's estate, his Glass House in New Canaan, on a glorious summer's eve. "We all drove up with Andy and Billy Linich to Connecticut, to perform. It was a benefit for the Merce Cunningham Dance Company." The evening was recorded by Andy in *Popism*. "Gerard was carrying his whip, because he would be performing. It was dark now, but the lights from inside the Glass House were shining on the trees and grass, and there were picnic baskets scattered all around. The Velvets were already starting to play, and Gerard rushed to join them." Sterling recalls that "that was a fond memory for all of us."

Meanwhile, discussions were taking place as to who should manage this magnificent four and Steve Sesnick emerged as the man. He had already been helping here and there, even out in Los Angeles, where he had club connections. Sterling says there were things about Steve that he didn't like, "but there were also unique problems with the whole idea of managing the Velvet Underground anyway. Traditional concepts wouldn't work. No one could make us play, which is why we didn't have an agent. We were always 'just about' to sign with William Morris or Ashley Famous, but we never did. We didn't like the percentages — we thought we should be a prestige account. These people have definite ways of putting together tours; we might have wanted to go out and play Chicago . . . and we might not; and if we didn't just then, we didn't go. But Steve Sesnick was the only person who was soliciting work for us.

"Sesnick had a lot going. He cared, and he worked. Billy said he thought he was the choice. So we agreed."

Moe also agrees. "Oh, I did like Steve Sesnick — we had a lot of fun together. The main reason he was real good is because he had so much faith in us. He was honestly convinced we could be the next Beatles. He always talked up — never down. Of course even I realised he was in it to get rich, also. But he was all for us, and he had such high, high hopes . . ."

Sesnick immediately got them an extended gig at the Boston Tea Party. At this point Nico dropped out. She had a solo commitment at Stanley's, on the Lower East Side, where she was performing with a single accompanist, though Sterling, John, Lou, Jackson Browne, Ramblin' Jack Eliot alternated weeks. "When we got the word from Sesnick, we invited her along," says Sterling. "'C'mon, Nico, no more screwing around here.' But she refused: 'Oh, nooooo, I have signed a contract, I *must* play here,' she said. Probably someone had told her, 'Oh you are so fabulous, but you'd better stay away from those wild, nasty boys.' She wanted to stay behind, so we said okay. She was *not* kicked out of the band. She simply wanted to try out the club format."

Some years later, Nico recalled her "dismissal" in more dramatic terms. "Everybody wanted to be the star," she assured Mary Harron in *New Wave Rock*. "Of course, Lou

Nico at "the Castle", Spring 1966 Archival Collection: Malanga

always was. But the newspapers came to *me* all the time. That's how I got fired — he couldn't take that any more. He fired me and then he fired John Cale. Have you met him? What do you think of him — sarcastic? He's incredibly quick. I'm very slow. But these weren't problems, because he wrote me songs that were slow, anyway. He wrote three very beautiful songs for me."

Moe brought it back to basics: "I was glad to see her go. To me, she was just a pain in the ass."

However Nico's departure put the Factory in a flap. Warhol, who considered the platinum blonde a star of the first magnitude, began losing interest with this bunch of renegades

when Nico had gone. The centre was not holding any more. The question came up as to who was really in command. John felt strongly that they'd worked constructively to capture something rare on the first album, but that the motivating spirit was gone. Erratic gigging for very little money was killing them. "And I felt," he told Amos Poe, "like a sideman, more or less. It was a mishandling of the situation." However although Cale felt demoralized, he did not think things were irreconcilable.

Lou felt otherwise. He summoned the band, minus Cale, to a summit conference at the Riviera Café in the Village and said Cale had to go. The decision was indefensible on musical grounds. Moe and Sterling reacted violently.

Lou with Andy Warhol *Ebet Roberts*

Sterling said, "I was enraged! To me it was unthinkable. I really laid into Lou." But Lou had made up his mind and when the heat was approaching white hot, he pulled his trump card — he would dissolve the Velvet Underground entirely. There was a silence.

"From the point of view of the band, it was tragic," says Sterling with vehemence fourteen years later.

"I never knew what the real problem was between those two," reflects Moe. "I felt John might consider he was a little restricted — because he is a major talent. Maybe he felt he wanted to do more on his own. We were not very close friends. He was the most distant . . . the most reserved. But I was so sad when he went. Musically, I missed him a great deal too, especially on *Heroin*. I always wished he was over there on stage. He had such a great input on the songs. He was such a major talent . . . oh, I *wish* they could've gotten along better!"

Sterling was sick about the whole thing. He was very close to John, and refused to break up the friendship. "It happened. There was no point in bringing it up again. There was a lot of tension because we were still hanging around together."

Without Cale, there would not be more than a faint frame to *White Light/White Heat*. The album is built around the power of his viola, organ and voice, the freedom of his in-creasing-intensity repetition concept, animal sounds and the approximation of old machin-ery falling from a very high height. It is uneven-ly recorded at best; the sound technician attempting to get this holocaust into grooves told them they were exceeding the power tolerance of the equipment. Nobody tuned down, least of all John, producing, said Sandy Pearlman in an early *Crawdaddy*, "this fan-tastic spectre of doom".

"The album", wrote Richard Cromelin, "car-ried paranoia into neurosis and further dimmed the line between love and violence. Breakdown time was approaching, disease progressing."

The basically crummy mix only highlighted the abrasiveness of the entire structure, which was a combination of a speed rush and a speed headache. It is the first of many Lou Reed albums to be dedicated to an all-amphetamine view of the world. *Sister Ray,* described by Lou in *Melody Maker* as "a graphic song", is a celebration of sailors, syringes and masturba-tion or sodomy. It became a favourite of War-hol, who told him, "Oh Lou, make sure that you make them do the 'sucking on my ding-dong' song." "So we did it. Seventeen minutes of violence . . . everyone was taken by surprise."

THE VELVET UNDERGROUND

"Oh, I was so sad when John went. I always wished he was over there, flailing away on his viola."

Moe Tucker

The third album was *The Velvet Underground*, a "grey", "acoustic", "religious" album, the polar antithestis of *White Light/White Heat*. Controlled, ascetic, whimsical and beguiling, it contains audible lyrics and even melodies one could hum, and a number of future "greatest hits". It also offered hints to those willing to decipher them of the path Lou Reed would eventually follow to personal survival, what Richard Meltzer called his "basically surburban structure".

The Velvet Underground follows the progress of the mental and physical anguish of Candy, as she moves into strength and the ability to go out and "find a new illusion". Like her creator, she must experience everything "to know completely/What others so discreetly talk about" and find her "proper place". The resolution is that there is no resolution, but there are a number of possibilities, and they might produce the person who tells her, "hello, you're my very special one" and end her alienation.

The album, like the band itself, moved out of anarchy into a sort of balance, with the inclusion of Doug Yule to replace Cale, on bass. Doug was a Boston boy who had played in the Grass Menagerie and often put up the Velvets in his apartment there. Sterling and Moe felt he was qualified and would work out technically, but that he clearly lacked any of the genius and intensity John brought to every song.

The album seemed to indicate the end of Lou's free-floating nihilism. Every song had a measure of hope, the possibility of redemption. Self-destruction was not the answer. "The anguish he was reflecting upon," says Danny Fields," was not his own. He was personalising what he'd seen. As an artist, he's kept his distance and refused to be destroyed by it. Oh, he'd had his ups and downs, but he's in no way a tragic figure. He simply had the brilliance to turn it all into art."

The songs reflect upon the wasted lives Lou had watched around him, the people searching for an answer in decadence and situations structured by other people's needs. "Nearly half the songs written in (the last three years) dealt essentially with bondage," asserts Richard Meltzer, "Most noticeably in *I'm Set Free*." In *Murder Mystery*, a life of momentarily gratifying chaos is explored. It had originally appeared as a long poem in the *Paris Review*. "When I did that song," he told Lester Bangs, "I dismissed decadence." The incoherence of shifting options is suggested by two voices telling stories at varying speeds, a song whose secrets are hidden on the printed page.

Pale Blue Eyes, a moony love song, became a classic for its single line of love's ambiguity: "Mostly you just make me mad." It violated Sterling's premise of violent, antagonistic rock and roll emerging from the natural tension within a band. He tried to maintain that tension by instigating a "tremendous paranoia because I was still hanging around with Cale."

The sweetest song, *Jesus*, a direct plea for salvation ("Help me in my weakness, for I've fallen out of grace") was decried as "pseudo-religious symbolism" by Lenny Kaye and a "crypto-anti-eastern-backlash" by Richard Meltzer.

Released in the spring of 1969, *The Velvet Underground* managed to alienate many of the faithful who were still trying to figure out *The Gift* and preferred a distorted viola yowl to a soothing acoustic chord and were also not prepared to take their philosophical guidelines from a group whose best songs were about smack, speed, despair, S/M and self-abuse. However it got the only radio play they had achieved as yet, especially for *Pale Blue Eyes* and *Beginning to See the Light*. Its intimacy and hints of salvation made a wonderful accompaniment to acid trips.

Many of Lou's very favourite people, pop music journalists, loved this album then, and cherish it beyond price now. Brian Cullman

Gerard Malanga during a performance of the Velvet Underground at The Trip, Los Angeles *Lisa Bachelis/Archival Collection: Malanga*

wrote: "There were wrong notes and incredibly sloppy solos (check *Pale Blue Eyes*), but there's not a false note to be found anywhere." Ellen Willis wrote in *Stranded*, "The Velvets bring it off — make us believe/admit that the psychic wounds we inflict on each other are real and terrible, that to scoff at innocence is to indulge in a desperate lie — because they never succumb to self-pity. Life may be a brutal struggle, sin inevitable, innocence elusive and transient, grace a gift, not a reward ('Some people work very hard/But still they never get it right'); nevertheless, we are responsible for who and what we become."

For over a year the band worked together fairly smoothly. Steve Sesnick got them gigs and tours, and their cult popularity on the coasts grew steadily.

But Mike Curb, then president of MGM, was ready to scrap the group. After three tempestuous years and a number of lawsuits, he made the statement on the corporate manifesto that, "Groups that are associated with hard drugs . . . are very undependable. They're difficult to work with, and they're hard on your sales and marketing people."

What the marketing types had ever done to hype the Velvet Underground is not readily apparent. Amidst announcements of mutual disappointment, the group parted company with their label. More lawsuits, as ever, ensued.

Whatever MGM's supportive failings, the label delivered three excellent albums that "yield up their treasure," wrote Richard Williams, an early stalwart, in *Melody Maker*, "only to a listener who is prepared to treat them with respect and intelligence."

And they were still so separate from the mainstream that no one thought to invite them to Woodstock.

LOADED

"Any one who had a heart/ They wander round and break it,
Any one who ever played a part/ They wouldn't turn 'round and hate it . . ."

Sweet Jane

The band was not long unloved. Performing for a glossy record company shindig at the Salvation Club, off Sheriden Square in Greenwich Village, they were accosted by their old admirer, Ahmet Ertegun, President of Atlantic Records. Sterling remembers that he wasted few words: "You guys still want to sign? No *Heroin* or any of that stuff." Sterling assured him that they were doing much straighter material and that they bathed regularly, and Ahmet quickly secured them onto the artists' roster at Atlantic. "Ahmet liked us a lot from the first, but he couldn't put up with the drugs on the first album, or *Venus in Furs.*"

Danny Fields was, as ever, on the front line of the action, having secured yet another job as a publicist and trendsniffer. "People think I brought them to Atlantic, but it was coincidence that I was working there. Their lawyers and reps went to Ahmet once they were free of the first label, and then he decided to do a record right away."

Unfortunately, the material for this could not be rescued from MGM, where there was a nearly complete album ready to go. This would become the legendary "lost" work, and various bootlegs now circulating claim to be from this period.

Loaded is the most accessible, danceable and uptempo album of the Velvet Underground, and their last. It gave the world the two powerful rockers, *Sweet Jane* and *Rock 'n Roll* and the euphoric *New Age*, intertwined with fifties rock and roll playfulness. It is as close to pure pop as the Velvets would ever get and as good-timey as the classic Beach Boys' *Help Me, Rhonda.*

It is the album Lou Reed later felt would have put him in the pantheon of pop greats, had it been released a few years down the line. Lacking both anguish and feedback, *Loaded* was indeed musically sound and cohesive, disguising the fact that the band was at each others' throats during the entire production. Sterling stormed out of the studio on more than one occasion as Lou and Doug fought at the sound board, driving one producer and then his replacement absolutely crazy.

One of the things that burnt them all out was the physical demand of playing and recording simultaneously. "Lou," says Sterling, "simply does not have that durable a voice. He was so ragged on some of the cuts that we either had to stop the production, or let Doug take over. But no one preferred to have Doug sing." Although Doug told Philip Milstein in *What Goes On* that he felt Lou's voice had been used on all the final mikes, Lou was very unhappy with *Sweet Jane* and *New Age,* believing them to have been severely edited. The accusations and counteraccusations went on for years.

"*Loaded* is incomparably the best mix of any of our albums," asserts Sterling. "Lou had no control over the mix, and if Geoffrey Haslam and Adrian Barbar (recording and re-mix engineers) were involved in such a 'conspiracy', why did the work come out sounding better than anything else?"

Moe appears only minimally on the album, as she was spending a lot of time at home in Long Island with her new daughter. This was her only departure from four years of steadfast devotion to the band; "I always felt the key to lasting with Lou was to be upfront, normal and sane – someone he could depend upon, with no ego problems. I honestly didn't realise he was having a difficult time that summer. But some things didn't affect me the way they did the rest of the guys."

Sterling noted that Doug was very definitely moving in, once he sensed the leader of the pack was not maintaining his razor edge.

Richard Meltzer remembers going up to the Atlantic offices for an early pressing of *Loaded* for review – and overhearing Steve Sesnick, in an adjacent office, sincerely discussing having Lou's voice entirely removed from the album.

Loaded, released in September in America, and seven months later in the UK, met almost universal critical approval although in his review in *Rolling Stone,* Lenny Kaye stated that while it is indeed a fine testament, "perhaps the explanation (for its lack of punch) lies in the fact that it was recorded before they undertook a summer-long engagement in Max's (Kansas City) upstairs." Indeed this album provided the basis for two further years of touring until the final ignominious fade-out on foreign soil.

Buying a new custom guitar *David McGough D.M.I.*

Joseph Sia

THE VELVET UNDERGROUND LIVE AT MAX'S

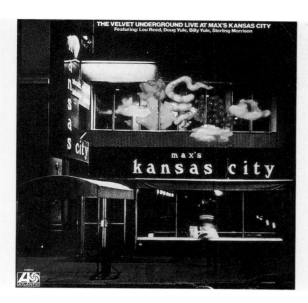

"The first band to do it live at the only prominent quasi-assfuck/pudsuck bar in town also to serve decent food (at least it was decent then)."

Richard Meltzer

Despite all the rumours of the problems the band was having, the Velvets' core cult remained faithful in New York. In the summer of 1970 Mickey Ruskin booked the band for a gig at Max's Kansas City, then at its legendary, Rome-before-the-fall level of glory. The multisexual hotspot on lower Park Avenue was getting a bit too popular, and approaching what Danny Fields termed "critical mass". But not yet! Max's was the nurturing gel of any trend or affectation approaching the socially amusing. "If you can score for sex and drugs in a place," said William Burroughs later on, "then you know you've really made contact."

The word got out fast — the Velvet Underground was playing the best music in the city, and the joint was packed. The band's bombast balance was diluted by the absence of Moe, who was back on Long Island with her first child, Kerry, but Lou gave perhaps the most euphoric performances of his career. "I'd never seen him so happy. He was cracking jokes, he was dancing!" remembers Billy Altman. Sterling and Doug Yule were in fine form; Doug brought his brother Billy in from Great Neck, where he occasionally played drums in high school.

Backstage, harmony vanished. Lou and Steve

Sesnick despised each other, largely on the grounds of style. Reportedly the manager told him to become more gregarious, more "showbiz", and make those groovy rock-star moves onstage. Lou felt this was contemptible. Doug told Philip Milstein that the manager finally snapped, "I don't care if you live or die" and Lou was very hurt. "It was sort of like a hard divorce," said Doug.

If true artistic transcendence occurs only in a hostile atmosphere, it was no wonder the backstage bitching produced such electrifying sets. Surrounded by the best and worst of his cohorts, recycled Warhol prettypartypeople and new, young idolators, Lou was friendly, freewheeling, and funny. Warhol film-maker Brigid Polk (or Berlin) brought in a cassette recorder and set it on her table close to the stage. It picked up two exuberant performances and some classic Sony-verité conversations . . . "Bill," said Lou, "get me a double Perrr-nod."

And so this first official bootleg which Brigid, urged on by Danny Fields, took to Atlantic Records and sold for five grand. Atlantic cleaned up a lot of the background buzz, but left in a sense of the joint's feel, to make listeners wish they had been there.

Max's is divided into rockers and ballads, the first side hurtling into *Waiting for the Man* and the merriest of *Sweet Janes*, nicely run out. Lou has said that the version of *Sweet Jane* on the later live album *1969 Velvet Underground* was the definitive one, but this is surely only a heartbeat below it. Sterling's scrappy guitar lines frame the beauty of Lou's voice on the chorus. If live recordings convey the excitement of the moment, this is a perfect example.

Ballads are *Sunday Morning, I'll Be Your Mirror, Pale Blue Eyes, Femme Fatale* and *Afterhours,* which Lou sang in place of Moe. As intense and friendly as the music is — Lou said later, "You can hear just enough" — it is supported by the sense of scene: the poses, the hysterical sexual circuitry, the drug fallout, and the poetry. Here's the best bar band of them all in their very best bar, projecting the most powerful *Beginning to See the Light* I've ever heard.

What was not recorded was the pressure which, that very night, drove Lou to pick up his guitar and walk out on the band for good. "Once something's over," said Danny Fields. "it's only a matter of minutes . . . and I don't think he ever really trusted Sesnick." It was August 23, 1970.

The moment was among the most painful for Lou Reed. The magnetic self-confidence and assurance that led him to (co-)found the band in the first place, and then forge radically original performances, was seriously thwarted for the first time. It was made sadder, happening behind the easy ebullience of a dancing crowd.

There wasn't much support from his fellows. Sterling's heart was not in the action by choice: "That year I was in City College summer school, which did not please Lou at all. I was studying Modern Drama and the Victorian Novel. Summer school is very short and intense; I was reading about thirty plays, and books like *Vanity Fair* and *Middlemarch* in the dressing room. I kept my guitar locked up in the office, arrived at night on my bicycle with my books, repaired to the dressing room, and read. Maybe I was insensitive to the situation. Really, I didn't care. We had been fighting for the previous year. I was still mad about John, and when I'm mad at someone, my approach is that I have nothing to say. After a while *you* have to figure out why I'm pissed off, because *I* won't tell you, and that leads to an examination of your life. No, I didn't stop talking to Lou – I just tuned him out completely and did whatever the hell I felt like.

"That jealousy . . . that was certainly a factor in John's demise . . . Lou could be jealous of everyone. It was my contention that he left the band when the magazine *Gay Power* reviewed the show and said I was the sexiest lead guitarist since Keith Richards, and Dougie was just as cute as a Christmas present under the tree. And this is supposed to be Lou's constituency! I said to Steve Sesnick, 'Boy, will Lou be hot when he reads this.'

"But after all this went down, Lou waited a while and came to my apartment, making overtures about how I should throw in with him." Lou had visions of a new band, definitely minus the Yule boys. Sterling was more interested in finishing his degree without hassles. "Maybe I should have done it," he told Mary Harron ten years later, but Sterling would stay with the Yule 'Velveteens' as writer Donald Lyons termed them, for another full year.

But the Velvets dragged on in one form or another for almost two years. Doug Yule told *Melody Maker* that he thought there'd been enough material for a double live album, but that the manager scotched it. Sesnick for his part did not display overwhelming sympathy. He whisked in Boston bassist Walter Powers and moved the ambitious Yule up to lead vocal and guitar. Doug swiftly appropriated Lou's exact phrasing and a fair imitation of his delivery, which along with his readiness to bad mouth Lou to the press, didn't exactly enhance his status within the band.

Completely alone, and savaged by drugs and betrayal, Lou moved back home to Freeport, managing to deal with lawsuits and accusations that followed his departure. He had been shaken by the internal warfare. One friend recalls visiting him some months after the Max's debacle, to encounter a quiet, mannerly suburban son in khaki pants who talked about his poetry. He recovered slowly, working as a typist in his father's Garden City accounting firm and 'realigning' himself, as he later described it.

Sterling continued to play with the band, completing an American tour in support of *Loaded*. But he had several applications in to colleges and universities to teach English Literature. One weekend when the Velvet Underground were playing in Houston he called the University of Texas at Austin only to find that he could begin his course the following Monday. And so he left.

By this time, Moe relates, Yule had become "a complete asshole with an ego you wouldn't believe." When he first came to the band at the end of '68, "we all thought he was great – a great guitar player, bass player, singer. But within a year he'd become an asshole . . . in my eyes, and I believe, in Lou and Sterling's. It was a lot of subtle things. If a new song came along, he'd be on bass, usually, with Sterling on guitar. Without being invited, Doug would pick up his guitar and start creating a part for himself. Many times Sterling would have to tell him, 'Hey, you're the bass player . . .'

"We all wondered why Lou would put up with this, for years. Why didn't he just say, 'I want him out of the band?' We were all so damned sick of him, we would've jumped on it. But he just let it build up . . . personally, I think the real reason he finally left was Doug. I didn't see this as a big plot on the part of Steve Sesnick. But yes, the moment Lou was gone, Steve clearly picked out Doug as the next 'star'. He took over the vocals and started writing some songs. There seemed to be a lot of ego-petting. Maybe he felt that Doug would simply be a lot easier to manipulate."

While Sterling was explaining the traumas of *Jane Eyre* to his first classes, Steve reached for another Boston rocker, Willie Loco Alexander,

then known as William, on keyboards. "I didn't want to join a ghost band," he remembers, "but they promised they'd change the name. I could record an album of my own stuff and see Europe and America." Moe squashed that idea. "We were the Velvet Underground . . . the only band *I* wanted to be in. After seven years I wasn't ready to turn around and be the Monkees. And no, that wasn't going to stop everyone from asking, where was Lou? Finally, I did leave, after Doug pulled so many stunts on the British tour I couldn't stand it. You know, that last album, *Squeeze,* was totally his little production. Walter and Willie were with us. They used to be his greatest fans, back in Boston. By the time the tour was over, they hated him so much they each said, 'I'll never play with that son-of-a-bitch again.'"

In October of 1971 Richard Williams reviewed a "so-called" Velvet Underground gig at London's Speakeasy. Casting journalistic objectivity to the winds, he declared that "What we saw that night was a travesty, a masquerade. It began with two pastiches of early Velvets songs, *Waiting for the Man* and *White Light/White Heat.* Yule's vocal fills on the latter

song reproduced Reed's recorded work exactly, which gave some indication of the lowly aims of this band . . . *Rock 'n Roll* was a disaster, one of Reed's finest songs speeded up and reduced to triviality."

It was during intense infighting, and counter-accusations that Doug and Sesnick convinced the rest of the band to return to America and the album *Squeeze* was produced. "When it all came down in London," wrote Willie Alexander, "ol' Dougie ended up making the album all by himself with Deep Purple's drummer. Moe and Walter and me went home, while Dougie stayed to mix the sonofabitch."

The greatest band in, as Lester Bangs would say, the history of the human eardrum, died on a somewhat pathetic note, crushed by an imbalance of talent and ego. But Lou's individual genius was not dimmed as the songs went on to become the largest collection of clasics by a single writer in rock and roll. "All I wanted to do," Reed later told Mikal Gilmore, "was to write songs that someone like me could relate to. At the worst, we were like antedated realists. At the best, we just hit a little more home than some things."

HOTEL
ONE BEDROOM SUITE FOR REED WITH WATERBED IF POSSIBLE
ONE SINGLE MILLER
THREE DOUBLES

REED SHOULD BE REGISTERED IN ALL HOTELS AS JOE SALINGER
GROUP SHOULD BE REGISTERED AS R MILLER GROUP
REMEMBER ISSUED TICKET FOR MILLER LEAVING UNITED STATES OCTOBER
10

Lou with Nico in Blakes Hotel, London, 1975 *Mick Rock*

LOU REED:
THE FIRST SOLO ALBUM

"What I liked in Lou Reed was a strong sense of humour, a dark, street-smart sense of humour. But all that changed."
Dennis Katz, Vice President of A&R, RCA

After months of suburban calm on Long Island Lou made tentative steps downtown towards his old haunts in the Big Apple. He read *Heroin*, a number of other Velvets favourites and some gay poems at St. Marks Church on the Bowery. He saw a few friends and gave the impression of being nervous, quiet, even apprehensive. His media companions Richard and Lisa Robinson determined that he should not squander himself on poetry readings, even poetry readings that were media events. They organized several social engagements at which Lou could once again encounter the rock cognoscenti, and Lisa hatched up a supportive guest list that managed to change his life in a few months.

These Robinson blowouts allowed Lou to mingle with music's movers and shakers, make himself visible, and sniff the wind. At one such event he met Dennis Katz, Director of Business Affairs at CBS. He also encountered the city's hottest rock critic Richard Meltzer, who was about as famous as he was at the time. Lou seemed impressed by the serious drinker whose street smarts and love of language kept the usual rock bullshit to a tolerable minimum.

Their most intimate confrontations occurred when Richard and girlfriend Roni Hoffman, Richard and Lisa and Lou and his date, a blonde named Betty, enjoyed "a sit-down dinner of chicken in cherry sauce concocted by Lisa's own hands."

"Lou," he remembers, "was just coming out of his cocoon. He'd been living with his parents, writing poetry and doing acoustic versions of songs into his tape recorder." Socially, he appeared in need of considerable coddling. "He'd feel terrible if the wrong thing was said, and he sensed he was at any sort of *disadvantage.* Then he'd strike back and actually get personally *nasty.* Even in general conversation, he'd be real . . . competitive."

Lou's companion Betty, who soon fell asleep on the rug, was a quiet, sane, normal blonde young woman, that Lou had apparently discovered on one of his endless shopping trips. "He'd decided the time was right for him to go hetero, and what could be more perfect than a blonde named Betty? She was just like Betty in the comic books. Lou used to needle her constantly about his gay past. When Betty fell asleep, it was Lisa's cue to zero in on this very subject. 'Lou – isn't bisexuality the best of both worlds?'

"Lou replied, 'No Lisa, it is not. Bisexuality is just a cop-out. I am cultivating heterosexual experiences because one cannot be bisexual – one is either straight or gay.' Lisa said she could dig it, and Lou seemed glad."

"Betty," he enthused in the magazine *Fusion*, "is not hip at all, and I want to keep her that way. I believe in pretty princesses." He also wrote a poem published in the same magazine with that same affirmation. He said it might make him a "bisexual chauvinist pig".

Perhaps sensing the commercial potential of all this reconsidered eroticism, RCA Records signed both Lou Reed and David Bowie to the label within months of each other.

The visionary behind this transaction was Dennis Katz, the new Young Turk in the RCA ranks. An unusual combination of corporate lawyer, rock rat and literary scholar, Katz was drafted as Vice President of A&R, because the label felt "I was musically oriented, and had an ability to negotiate and structure deals that would give them an A&R head with both backgrounds. An A&R head must be able to do more than evaluate acts and listen to tapes. He must have a feeling for an act's commercial potential, to know what they'll be worth."

On Dennis' "first and last" A&R job he signed both Lou and David, which the label happily backed. He saw outstanding potential in Lou. "Up to that point, he was basically a songwriter. I really liked the Velvet Underground,

even if I became familiar with their work only after they disbanded. The original group with John Cale had a much wider effect on other artists, but the later band was much more commercial, in my opinion. *Loaded* is by far their most commercial album, but neither Nico nor John are there. I liked both categories of Velvets very much.

"What I enjoyed particularly about Lou Reed was a strong sense of humour, a dark, street-smart sense of humour. I would come to change my mind about this and see little humour in Lou's work from that point on. No songs to compare with *Sweet Jane* or *Rock 'n Roll* or *Lonesome Cowboy Bill*. I don't think he ever again made a statement as significant as *Heroin*. When I got to know him, I sensed that the qualities I'd first seen in him changed, and the humour wasn't there. Oh, there was some of that hard-edged humour in the *Transformer* album, later on. I simply do not enjoy his music the way I used to."

At the time Katz seemed to have ultimate faith in him as an artist. By all accounts Lou seized upon Dennis as a father figure, even though the two were roughly the same age. Poised, literate, happily married and devoted to his career, Dennis represented a masculine strength Lou never found at Max's. Everyone around the two recalls their deep friendship with some awe, especially since Lou, for years, did nothing to contradict or challenge him in any way.

Now that he was signed to a major, the artist needed a manager. He approached his beloved Danny Fields. Danny had a sometime philosophy of trying anything once. But in no time "it just became too much to handle. Now, everything about his career was in exploratory stages. I decided this was best left to professionals who weren't so emotionally or aesthetically involved, who weren't so enraptured of him. He was making me crazy. So at a party at the Robinsons', I went over and told him, 'Lou, I love you, but this won't work. I just want to be your friend.'"

Lou then definitely decided on Richard Robinson, then under contract to RCA, as his producer. Robinson, whose Renaissance gifts had gained cult acceptance by his handling of the Flamin' Groovies and Hackamore Brick albums, considered Lou his overriding obsession of the time. "To date," he told Henry Edwards in *After Dark*, "He has not been recorded in a way that enables him to communicate easily with those who wanted to

listen. And he's written the best rock and roll songs I've ever heard."

Lou, Richard and Lisa left for Morgan Studios in North London in the first month of 1972 with a batch of old Velvets material and new poems composed during Lou's period of "exile and great pondering", as he described it in his RCA bio.

The resulting record was charming but uneven, a beguiling stand-off between sensitive ballads and rockers that would have been eaten alive by three bars of *Sister Ray*. They would perhaps have been hits from anyone else. Robinson's production was meticulous but sterile, just one step above a poetry reading, and many reviewers found the result unsatisfying. He had done precisely what he announced he would do, but most listeners put it down and rushed to put the *Banana* album back on the turntable.

After the experience with Morgan Studios, Lou began, and never veered from, his custom of using the best musicians money could grab. A bunch of "technically competent British session cats," as Lester Bangs described them, had accompanied him in London. "I mean these guys are good," lamented Gary Kenton in *Fusion,* "but they are strictly back-up. Very clean and distant." They would all go on to distinguish themselves: Caleb Quaye, Rick Wakeman, Steve Hough and Paul Keogh, but where the brawling Velvets forged into a single subatomic unit behind him, these people — no matter how well-accredited — simply had good manners. Lou didn't relate to them at all.

Whoever gave Lou the idea of trying to "sing" on this offering had him reaching for notes and vocal styles that he could not accommodate. What John Rockwell termed his "limited, insecure baritone" made him the most compelling of rhythmic poets, but also meant that he would never master the quasi-Vegas "sincerity" he seemed to be striving for here. Robinson's production, unfortunately, did not cover this up with shock waves of feedback. "Reed's voice," noted Richard Cromelin, "Needs a dynamo, like the one the Velvet Underground provided, kicking him from behind all the way."

For all this, the production did provide a charming glimpse of Lou Reed at his most adolescent; many of the songs have a whimsical vulnerability that even *Loaded* would have given a boogie backbeat. Sterling Morrison found the work "derivative and not very good". The song *Walk & Talk It* seems lifted

whole from the early pages of *Last Exit To Brooklyn,* the fine *Wild Child* has a debt to Dylan's hippie heroines, while the opening *I Can't Stand It* could possibly be an oblique tribute to the creator of *Yackety Yak.* But who cares? Even an uncertain, hesitant Lou Reed is far better than the martyred ghost of a shattered cult hero. It was very good to have him back. Donald Lyons, in a swoon of nostalgia, wrote in *Interview* that he is "a classic romantic — the smell of his work is the smell of Baudelaire's Paris — grappling, tempted and sometimes happy, always human. It's a wonderful album."

Robert Christgau gave it a B+ in his *Village Voice* Consumer Guide. "Reed is everything a singer-songwriter should be — sentimental, subtle and humorous vocally." But he did not consider that this compared with the Velvets. Missing, perhaps, were "two or three great songs — maybe a stronger rhythm mix."

"Edith Piaf he ain't," noted Lester Bangs in *Creem,* describing his moody cabaret delivery of the song *Berlin,* in which he describes an encounter with a Nico-lookalike ("five foot ten

THE PAUL DAINTY CORPORATION PRESENTS

LOU REED IN CONCERT

inches tall") and slinks off with her to a "small café" with "candlelight and Dubonnet on ice". Just as the listener is about to go into insulin shock, Lou sneaks in "Don't forget/Hire the vet/He hasn't had that much fun yet" which John Cale for one thought he meant most earnestly: "He's dead serious. He'll be getting really passionate about something, and you'll burst out laughing, and he'll go 'Are you crazy? That's not *funny!*' And he'll get offended . . ."

This was the first appearance of *Berlin,* which would have its own album in another two years; Lou would eventually visit the city on a triumphal concert tour in 1979, after having put it on the map in the American musical consciousness. He would pronounce it unremarkable, except for the Wall. *Berlin* was the favourite track of Reed tracker Richard Williams in *Melody Maker:* "Lou's never been there, but he uses his knowledge of Nico as a filter for his feelings about the city. The verses have a candlelit, nightclub atmosphere."

The album closes with an abbreviated *Ocean* which was done with much more feeling on the live double album *1969 Velvet Underground Live,* but which is nonetheless full of studio splashing noises, and very engaging for its sense of place and physical release, which may also partially derive from Delmore Schwartz's perfect *Far Rockaway.*

In the spring of 1972 Lou, Nico and John Cale performed at Paris' Bataclan Theater. "I always wanted to do a real night club torch song," he explained in *Circus,* "and you know, I didn't play at all. John Cale played piano and I sat on a stool with my legs crossed. During the instrumental break I lit a cigarette . . ." Nico had let her hair go back to its original auburn and announced that she was no longer in her "mellow blonde" period. John had now produced, arranged and played on three albums for Nico, *Chelsea Girl, The Marble Index* and *Desertshore.* To balance her Wagnerian sense of futility, doom, loss, and pathological misery, he also produced the Stooges from Detroit.

Lou returned to the US and engaged a curious garage band from Yonkers, the Tots, to back him on tour. Singularly talentless, but terribly excited to be playing with a real superstar, they followed him around the country to universal pans. Lou fired and rehired them with some regularity, finally sending them back down the Henry Hudson Parkway for good when he started getting gigs in larger venues, where crowds might do them actual bodily harm.

TRANSFORMER

LOU REED-TRANSFORMER

"God knows rock & roll could use, along with a few other things, some good faggot energy . . ."

Nick Tosches, Rolling Stone

"Of course the Factory was one big tangle of unsortable assholes, but the record buying public was not exactly keeping pace."

Ed McCormack, Changes

RCA Records was not happy. With the luke-warm response to his first solo album, Lou's future with the label looked shaky, at best. "Because of minimal sales, I really had to go to bat for him, in terms of a second album," remembers Dennis Katz. Happily, help was hovering in the wings. David Bowie, also signed to RCA by Katz, never failed to praise Lou and the Velvets as inspirational sources and he often included *Waiting for the Man* and *White Light/White Heat* in his stage show with the Spiders from Mars. Lou's first British appearance had been with David at the Royal Festival Hall in the summer of '71 where the Long Island son was electrifying, in spangles and layered eye liner.

Bowie wasted no time in proposing to the label that in fact *he* was the one to produce the second album.

The label thought that was great. "They had a lot of faith in Bowie," says Dennis, "because he produced both *Hunky Dory* and *Ziggy Star-dust*. So they were then willing to take another shot on an album – assuming *he* was working with Lou. They made it clear that they were disappointed in Lou. But I thought he still had

tremendous potential – we hadn't *begun* to tap it. I fought with the marketing people and the sales people who kept pointing out, 'What are we doing wasting our time with a guy who sold six or seven thousand albums?' The pressure *I* was under, at the time, was from the purely commercial point of view. They rejected the direction – and specifically the production – of the first album. But if David took over – they could accept that. And I was wholeheartedly for that. The production did not come out the way I'd anticipated it, either; it was much too sparse."

David was fast approaching international superstardom. Where Lou described, or mostly alluded to, various sexual compulsions in his songs, Bowie, heavily 'encouraged' by his radically original management company, Mainman, fleshed out his creations from the centre of his own kaleidescope. At that time the uncontested hero and lust object of bisexually chic London, he vamped David-as-Ziggy into the front line of fame. With electro-shock orange hair, blood-black nail polish, lots of skin, and clinging lurex costumes that ne'er obscured a curve, he was Eros as Androgyne. Gay, straight or bi, he was simply Desire, and his magnetism more than impressed the Phantom of Freeport, who'd done it all on jeans and black leather. The notion that David would repudiate the entire image as a creatively calculated crock of shit was not even a tear in a press agent's eye, as yet.

The rampaging Ziggy cult, which seemed to lure all Britain out of the closet, outdazzled even the drag queens around Warhol, whose charms had been appreciated by only a few from select blocks of Village turf. Ziggy's sexual fireworks and stripper's tricks appeared at precisely the right time and plateau of boredom in British rock. Plus which, the record business has rarely seen the likes of the publicity machine behind him: Mainman, run by David's manager, Tony DeFries, and featuring the most passionate of publicists, Cherry Vanilla, would stop at nothing to get media attention for their notorious prodigy.

"Bowie was so *exciting*," said Cherry a decade later, "that we were out to prove him to the world! I confess we did use very basic techniques. But Tony DeFries always encouraged us to use our imaginations and do whatever we were best at! It was just – the right chemical combination. You know, people would work for us for *nothing*. When I think back to those early shows – the immense theatricality that no one had ever included in rock before David, that flamboyance – no wonder Lou was en- thralled by him! We all were.

"We would do anything to get him known. Once I called up a heavy AM disk jockey I'd slept with many years back, because I wanted to get his single, *Starman,* into the top 40. The guy said to me, 'Oh isn't David Bowie that faggot?' I said 'Why no, but even if he was, the song's from *Ziggy,* about a little spaceman. Couldn't you listen, without prejudice, for old time's sake? And he put it into his top 40 which was top exposure for *many* cities. If there was some disk jockey in, oh, Cincinnati who was halfway cute – and I knew by fucking him he would put David's record on the air, I fucked him. Then I'd hype my image, and pretend I'd fucked every *one* of them. Really, we made the whole thing up as we went along.

"*Transformer* was a very beautiful, very widely accepted album that David did out of love for Lou. Much later on ... I think it was during the *Diamond Dogs* days ... he and Lou spent the whole night carrousing and David said something like, 'That man is the devil. I'm never going to see him again.' But you know, David is so changeable, the next day he could be enthralled with the devil. They were close friends for so long ..."

Mainman pioneered two new concepts in publicity: the lavishly produced fantasy videos that are now the staple for artist promotion, and the intimate, sexually suggestive interview that made screaming headlines but still main- tained mystery because it didn't really *say* any- thing. Without the enormous allure of David Bowie, none of this silliness would have worked; indeed, "we tried it again with Johnny Cougar, and it failed miserably," says Cherry.

What this meant to one Lou Reed hot for commercial success was that all his midnight rambles could run loose in his art; finally, the world was catching up with him. "If I'd put out those first (Velvets) albums now, they'd be *hits,*" he told more than one interviewer. But most of the homosexuality in the Velvets material is either ambiguous or drowned in an orgiastic viola meltdown. *Lady Godiva's Operation* concerns surgery, but of what sort? It could be referring to transsexual restyling but then it could equally apply to an abortion, an hysterectomy or even the removal of a gall bladder. It just isn't clear. However after *Ziggy* had paved the way, Lou could kick open the closet door and unsnap the make-up case, camp up his already fey vision as voyeur of the sixties and make it *big.*

Lou at the Cafe Royal with Mick Jagger, David Bowie and Lulu, July 4, 1974 *U.P.I. photo*

In August of 1972 Bowie and Lou entered Morgan studios with guitarist Mick Ronson, who had worked closely with David on many projects. Who was hustling whom at the time is still being debated; some felt David was using the process to get close to Lou's creative genius and figure out just how he wrote *Heroin.* Others say Lou was simply dazzled by David, his management machine and his hysterical, absolutely enviable popularity. Anyway, it was a real love feast. "There are just two Bowie albums," Lou told Scott Cohen in *Circus,* "Hunky Dory and Ziggy – Ziggy is perfection. There's nothing wrong with it."

Transformer, Lou's second solo album was co-produced with Mick Ronson; both he and Bowie were given arrangement credit with Lou. The work is heavily Warhol-influenced, only this time accessibly so. The sharp but offbeat rocker, *Vicious,* the lyrics of which he later credited to Andy's observations as they walked around town one afternoon, offers the engaging lines:

When I see you walking down the street
I step on your hands and mangle your feet.

Andy's Chest, relating to the ghastly shooting of Warhol by Valerie Solanis at the Factory, is a childlike nonsense song of rearranged anatomy; which like so many of his songs, has a disturbing aftertaste. "His lyrics," Richard Williams wrote in a review of a Velvets album, "were designed to make the listener think hard."

Warhol contributed most of the players that Lou immortalized in his uncoy classic, *A Walk on the Wild Side.* Once again he plays a subtle role, this time a sort of Louis In Nighttown, coolly observing an explicit assortment of drag queens and hustlers Andy made into stars. "This is it – the song that started it *all*!" he would hail it in future concerts: indeed, it did put the solo career of Lou Reed into gear at last. *Wild Side* set forth the erotic antics of Holly Woodlawn, Candy Darling, Jackie Curtis and Joe D'Allesandro, who "never once gave it away". Lou's insinuating, jazzy hipster rap sent critics into a swoon; a review in *Coast* said the song "summed up all (he's) tried to do since he was Pasha of Pasha and the Prophets."

The very first transvestite rock offered to middle America, it featured three further lyrical innovations: oral sex, "coloured girls" and Valium. All three were considered grave errors in any calculations involving radio play – but not nearly as anti-social as *Heroin* or *Sister*

Ray, which no AM programmer even considered. Referring to one's backup group, the Thunder Thighs, as "coloured girls" was merely considered poor taste, not an assault on the American Way. The back cover, too, broke new ground, with Lou's cherished tour manager/art director Ernie Thormahlen posing as both butch and femme, the former handsomely enhanced by the addition of a not overly ripe banana diagonal to the inseam.

The album and its natural single *A Walk on the Wild Side* leapt out of the closet and onto the charts, the album soaring to #29 in the US in April of 1973. Where it made him many new fans, it also angered some of the faithful; he was their beautiful leather boy, bi, maybe, but what was all this swishy shit about eye-liner? But they came to realise that the best Lou Reed albums had something to offend almost everyone, in some way.

Ever since the suggestion that "you'd better hit her" snarled out from *There She Goes Again* on the first Velvet Underground album, Lou Reed has been accused of misogyny. The theme that women are trouble has indeed run through his work; they hurt you, they betray you, they run off with your friends, "mostly (they) just make you mad." Behind the evident frustration is their allure – otherwise why not unconditionally dismiss them. So much of his work is full of pain and rage that it seems a cheap shot to label him a woman-hater. Nevertheless, there are plenty of lines like

"But if'n you think that you get kicks
    from flirting with danger
Then kick her in the head
    and rearrange her."

Which hardly endeared him to the likes of readers of *Ms.* magazine.

Steve Chappel and Reebee Garofalo railed in *Rock 'n' Roll Is Here To Pay* that, "the last few years have seen the emergence of out-front homosexual musicians. However, the movement that was promised in the early David Bowie albums, especially *Hunky Dory,* toward a more honest treatment of male and female sexuality and homosexuality and toward a gentleness in emotional relationships was soon betrayed by Bowie and numerous camp followers, who began to sell sexual ambiguity as a commercial thrill. Most performers who were gay, like Lou Reed, simply lied about their homosexuality, and worse, continued to write songs degrading to women."

The desperation of the human condition was his recurring theme – almost everyone was

M. McKenzie

53

guilty. When asked by Howard Bloom in *Circus* when he started writing gay songs, he said, "Listen to the lyrics of my early songs. *Lady Godiva's Operation* was about a transsexual. And *Sister Ray* was about a gay dealer." No matter how sordid the battles of the sexes in his song, he always held out hope of communion. The almost excruciatingly tender *Perfect Day* is a description of a loving afternoon between two hopeful people getting joy out of ordinary pleasures.

Transformer became a staggering success. On April 21, 1973 *Walk On the Wild Side* (a cleaned up version — but many DJ's preferred to play the album cut) hit #16 on the US singles charts, and a month later #10 in the UK; whereas the album went to #13 in Britain. The Bowie/Ronson influence was considered paramount in the direction of the work. "Thanks to their intelligence and taste," Tim Jurgens wrote in *Fusion,* "Lou Reed has found the perfect accompaniment to such flights of fancy that he's been lacking since John Cale went his own way." The *Village Voice* noted that, "you can cut the atmosphere surrounding each song with a knife . . . and the clue to this album's appeal lies in . . . a mix that has a chance of startling the listener and touching our common humanity."

Lou assaulted several British venues, where his association with Bowie and Mainman, combined with his own hard-core audience of Velvet freaks, made him a genuine star. This was not unnoticed by Tony DeFries, who would spend (at least) three years trying to convince Lou to sign with him. "He was always running around telling people he was my manager, which he wasn't," Lou told Michael Watts, "although he tried."

On February 1, 1973 he made his US solo concert debut at Alice Tulley Hall; he was, by all accounts, electrifying and fully established himself as a local boy who had made good. He wore black leather jeans and jacket and seemed to have left glitter back in London. Everyone was still asking all those questions about his sex life, though, even though by this time he had married the "blonde and bland" Betty and moved to yet another high-rise haven on the Upper East Side. Some of Lou's lifelong supporters, who'd already shown their disapproval with comments like "Betty Boop" and "Betty — like with Archie and Veronica" were now deeply affronted that he would do something so disgustingly bourgeois and risk *losing his edge*. Drugs, sex, sleeplessness, Johnny Walker Black and rampaging brawls in leather bars were considered important to the private life of a true artist, but *marriage* . . .

The adoration he and Bowie felt for each other began to suffer, but only temporarily. Each dropped hints to a panting press that the other was exploiting the relationship. Bowie, for example, insinuated that Lou was borrowing too much of his identity, and Lou retaliated by calling him "a very nasty person, actually", in *Circus*. But the spat didn't last, and the two remained intensely involved throughout their careers, caring so desperately that it once reached the point of public physical violence.

Looking back on this period and at the respective talents of the two men Dennis Katz feels that "In retrospect, Lou Reed is more important — in terms of the influence he's had on other artists. But from a creative point of view, and a commercial point of view, Bowie is the artist I have more feeling for. David has been an excellent songwriter, an excellent vocalist and an excellent producer. He has also been extremely intelligent in directing his career, whether on his own or through others. I see him developing as a very important actor. All of these qualities attracted me to him, initially, as an artist. His whole posture was much more rounded, and far reaching, than Reed's."

Lou, for his part, was indebted to David for taking modern sexuality, in lyrics and lifestyle, anywhere he damned pleased and in any medium that amused him. For while journalists were falling over themselves surmising whether he really did live with that occult subcult of devil worshippers in that chic London suburb, Lou suddenly announced that the subject that *really* interested him at the moment was suicide.

BERLIN

"Awright, wrap up this turkey before I puke."
Bob Ezrin, producer.

"The smart thing to do now," the artist was heard to calculate, weighing the instincts of his newly receptive international audience, *"would be to hand them down a boogie album."* Instead he forged what is still held by many to be his solo masterwork, *Berlin*. Lugubrious and orchestral, almost Wagnerian, it concerns two amphetamine misfits in that divided city who drive each other and their children to unhappy ends.

Berlin is an expansion of the song in solo album #1, which may have concerned the experience of knowing Nico, who grew up 100 kilometers to the south. Surely her Teutonic high romanticism and predilections for doom were irresistible inspiration to an American rock and roller trying to cut away from his roots. However it is another one of Lou's secrets whether Nico's compulsions, which could include multi-national sexual and chemical experiments, were included into those of Caroline, the album's anti-heroine. At one point he intimated that "Caroline" lived in New York, didn't have children, but did have suicidal tendencies.

Caroline has Nico beat twenty times over, though, when it comes to self-destruction. A blonde, beautiful, aspiring actress, she meets her American husband by the Berlin Wall, bears him two daughters, and proceeds viciously to destroy their lives. Growing ever more independent, willful and compulsive, she tells her husband — the narrator, the role assumed by Lou — of his failure as a lover and a man. She makes *Wild Side's* Candy Darling look like a frigid feminist, slip-sliding through every form of sex the city has to offer; "the black Air Force sergeant was not the first one." She does a whole mess of drugs and then looks around for more trouble to get into. Raging with pain, the narrator locks himself into impotence. He is the victim — "And I'm the water boy?" — looking on at "that miserable fucking rotten slut couldn't turn anyone away." In the most harrowing song of the album *The Kids*, Caroline has her daughters taken away by a Responsible Agency (the sex police?), and their sobs build with the band into a wail of symphonic pain. Rage, brutality, betrayal and suicide follow, in terms so vivid many fans could not make it all the way through. "It may be," considered Lester Bangs, "the grandest dreariness you ever heard."

The emotional intensity of the album is maintained by the production and arrangement talents of Bob Ezrin. Ezrin was the young Toronto studio wonderboy behind Flo and Eddie and Alice Cooper, whom he launched into the mainstream with *I'm Eighteen*.

Contacted by business manager Dennis Katz, Ezrin discussed with Lou the concept of an album built entirely around movie images, a "film for the ears". Lou "agreed to write a story and create a character around himself." The idea was so fully actualized that they "shot stills from this nonexistent movie that'll be included with the lyric booklet" Ezrin told *Rolling Stone*.

The two then lined up Lou's most powerful band since the early Velvets, with Stevie Winwood on keyboards, Jack Bruce on bass, Aynsley Dunbar and B.J. Wilson on drums, and Cooper session guitarists Richard Wagner and Steve Hunter. Lamenting in the *Daily News* that the original song *Berlin* "wasn't done right, and I was very sad about it," Lou nonetheless found himself with the full complement of outstanding musicians. For once, rock's most compelling voyeur/raconteur found himself with a producer who could substantiate the power of his images.

The project became something of a cause and a personal obsession. Lou had convinced RCA of the commercial potential of the album, telling them "how astute it would be to follow up *Walk On The Wild Side* with not just another hit single but with a magnificent whatever. I shoved it through." Musicians working in the studio ten hours a day are less easy to jive. Recording once again in London, to avoid being forced to use the RCA Studios in New York, Lou watched his superstar sidemen fall under the spell. "Jack Bruce," he recalled, "wasn't supposed to be on the whole thing, but he went through the whole trip because he liked it a lot."

In Ezrin, Lou found his most fanatical acolyte. For fourteen and twenty hours a day, Ezrin correlated technology and talent, until he went completely over the edge. After three weeks he had to be put away in a quiet place where the only tracks were those made by birds on the windowsill. "I got home and I started breaking things. It literally drove me crazy. I couldn't control myself," he later told Steven Gaines. "Doing that album," said Lou, "did have its effect on Bobby."

"Here's where Bobby blew it," analyzed one Anonymous Observer. "He played the wrong game with Lou – he tried to be brilliant, to be his match. Nobody could ever be as brilliant as Lou. The only way to survive is to be the best you can and care for him deeply and hope nothing goes horribly wrong."

Berlin was released in 1973, and immediately drew violent reviews, of which "the worst album by a major artist in 1973" was one of the more restrained. Rolling Stone pronounced it "a disaster". The New Musical Express found it a sleazefest "that will culminate in a breathtakingly vulgar pair of concerts at London's Rainbow." "It is heterosexual," noted William Gurvitch in the Village Voice, "but about a druggy bi slut who gets her children taken away." Even Bangs, devoted to Lou all of his adult life could pronounce it only "the most disgustingly brilliant album of the year."

"I have difficulty caring about Reed's maladjustment," lamented another critic. Bruce Malamut considered it "the most naked exorcism of manic depression ever to be committed to vinyl." David Downing wrote in Future Rock that it contained "no hope . . . (The protagonists) stare straight into each other's eyes, and find only emptiness." And Roger Klorese regretted the range of Lou's vocals, "which sound, typically, like the heat-howl of the dying otter."

Some were moved to the point of rage, Stephen Davis expanding that "certain records are so patently offensive that one wishes

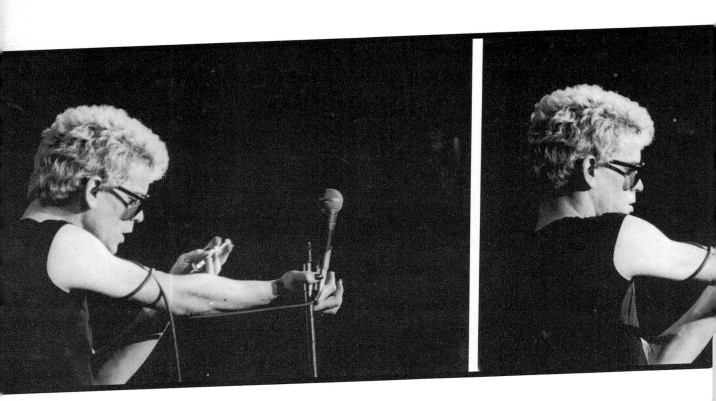

to take . . . physical vengeance on the artists that perpetrate them . . . Goodbye, Lou.''

New York glitter chick David Johanson, who owed much of his sequinned street approach to the success of *Transformer,* saw it in geographical terms: "I know why he called it *Berlin.* If you called it Seattle or Cleveland you couldn't write a story about it, because everybody would know . . . but if you give an American kid a flash like Berlin, that's something very exotic, and you can say anything because he's never been to Berlin and he won't know you're bullshitting him.'' But he found the album itself "a hoot – I hope he gets away with it. It's very vindictive, very moralistic – I like that.''

Lou was always the darling of the critical elite, most of whom were his age and had their sensibilities forged in the heat of the Velvet Underground. They could never dismiss him, always stood quick to forgive, and were the first to spot any poetic shard of Enduring Beauty. Paul Nelson called the album "unforgettable in many ways . . . and probably underrated.'' But John Rockwell of the *New York Times* was the most perceptive of all, terming it "one of the strongest, most original

rock records in years,'' and lauding the poetic and theatrical impulses that informed the work.

In November 1973, RCA released the single *How Do You Think It Feels* and Lou headed for the hills of Stockbridge, Massachusetts to rehearse for the hour, maintaining Hunter and Wagner and their guitars, and including Ray Colcord on piano and Peter Walsh on bass. His business manager, Dennis Katz, primed the press by promising "a new, colourful show that will be theatrically shocking''. John Rockwell stated that "his show at the Academy of Music on December 21 should be an event.''

How Do You Think It Feels was no *Wild Side* in terms of popularity, although a fine rocker. It also contained enough all-purpose catch phrases, like many of his most "popular'' songs, to appeal to a wide segment of his audience. It did not require a major drug habit to hook into the regretful realism of "Hunting around always/'Cause you're afraid of sleeping/How do you think it feels/To always make love by proxy.'' Too many of us are hunting around too much of the time to not connect with this.

The album crept slowly up the US charts but actually made it to #7 in Britain by the end of

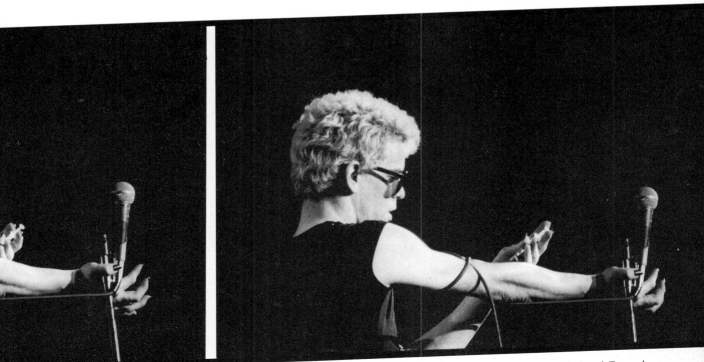

Shooting up in Winterland *Michael Zagaris*

57

October. Sales were perfectly respectable for a normal artist, but following the blaze of *Transformer*, they appeared a disaster.

During the critical assaults on *Berlin*, Lou had decided that almost all rock critics were his natural enemies. They complained that he had sold out his arty cult roots when *Wild Side* was commercially successful. When he returned to a more complex and deeply felt style, they complained that he was no fun, and much too neurotic to relate to everyday life. "Who cares about critics?" was one of his more printable replies. "*Berlin* was an album for adults."

Some critics came to change their minds about *Berlin*. The album has been judged a sort of masterpiece, and there has been a steady demand for its re-release. Rare copies fetch about $45 in oldies emporiums. Its songs and

who met her commented on her niceness and her all-American short blonde hair. Many felt that she had tried to build a cozy nest for Lou, from which he would not be compelled to stroll to the liquor store every night.

"For a while," his friend Ed McCormack wrote in *Changes,* "it seemed like self-preservation, but eventually he realised it was the worst thing in the world. The girl he had married wasn't trying to save him — she was trying to housebreak him." Yet during their marriage many had commented on how much more at peace with himself Lou seemed. Others were pissed at the possibility of their favourite leather boy, closet queen, drug fiend, apostate of anarchy and whatever other black sheep Lou had been impersonating losing his edge. When he commented in interviews that certain segments of his audience felt they owned him, he had it nailed.

At any rate, Lou tucked his dragon's tail into his leather jeans and headed out on tour, ready to give his fans the fearsome rock and roll they clearly desired above all else.

The morose, powerful songs of the *Berlin* album and Ezrin's intricate arrangements lodged in his heart. Later on Lou would incorporate *Caroline Says, Oh Jim, Men of Good Fortune, The Kids* and *Sad Song* into his stage show. "*Berlin* was a big flop, and it made me very sad," he told a packed house at New York's Bottom Line five years later. "I warn you now, this is the depressing part of the show . . ." Some of his rowdier later audiences, depressingly, are most roused by the rage of "Anyone else would have broken both of her arms . . ." without considering the careful characterization that precedes it.

The florid cinematic images of *Berlin* impressed lifetime admirers. Andy Warhol announced his desire to make it into a musical comedy starring Lorna Luft, though the project has gone unrealised. So has Lou's hope, expressed in *Melody Maker* later, that Roman Polanski make a nice decadent movie. "And I've been waiting for someone to make it into an opera . . ."

The album has an eerie legacy. It helped to create the image of Berlin city as a wellspring of artistic inspiration. The icy synthesizer rock coming out of the superb studios there lured experimenters like Iggy Pop, David Bowie and many others to take up residence. Lou didn't need the place. "The whole thing is just a fantasy."

emotions have stood the test of a decade. The man was always ahead of his time.

The emotional devastation of the album was not confined to its audience. Even as Bob Ezrin recovered from studio psychosis, his personal life suffered. And then Betty left Lou. General opinion is that Betty was a sane, right thinking person who could not understand the obsession with drugs, despair and suicide. Those

ROCK N ROLL ANIMAL
1969 VELVET UNDERGROUND LIVE

Circus magazine: Do you have a nickname?
Lou: *Butch.*

In the late autumn of '73, before his marriage broke Lou and Betty set out across America with his blazing band of medium-to-heavy metal marauders. Playing large auditoriums, with the guitar pyrotechnics of Hunter and Wagner blasting off the walls, he fired up new legions of fans that could only be baffled by *Berlin.* But he aroused responses in some audiences that were very unpleasant. Fans would try to grab him, hit him or strip him — one managed to bite him on stage in Buffalo. Stage security began to assume major importance in any performance. His image seemed a catalyst for violent extremes and stupid destruction. As his popularity soared, his audiences became so volatile that eventually he refused to play any large venue in the United States.

"Morbid, self-destructive, obsessive . . . there has always been an atmosphere surrounding his musical activities, both live and recorded," noted one 'Minor Wisdom' in *Fusion.* The *Berlin* tour was the apotheosis of this premise. Physically, a relatively robust Reed led into it in stunning black leathers, whiteface, Biba black nail polish and matching lipstick, black eyeliner and long, curly locks. He looked like a sexy, rabid wolverine. Within a few weeks his hair had been shorn into a crew-cut iron cross and he resembled an upwardly-mobile member of the Hitlerjugend. Poor diet had made his figure lean; around this he wrapped bicycle chains and heavy buckles from bondage

boutiques such as Greenwich Village's Pleasure Chest. All this provoked a lot of free-floating hostility, reducing any communication to the basics, which is really what the electrifying *Rock n Roll Animal* is all about.

Around this time he became close friends with Dennis' brother, Steve Katz, star guitarist with Blood, Sweat & Tears. An accomplished musician and a true fan, he meant more than good company to Lou. "Working with him," recalls Steve, "eased me out of the unhappiness with my own band. When he asked me to produce his next album, I went for it."

Together Dennis and Steve considered the fate of *Berlin,* "a beautifully crafted album that was bombing . . . I think it sold maybe 20,000 copies. I told Lou we'd have to get rid of his old mystique and put out his songs to new people. He had a great band now, and he could become a star with a hot live album." Lou approved the strategy.

Steve had spent his formative years as guitarist for the Blues Project, a band whose lyrical stance was the opposite of the Velvet Underground's sordo-rock. "We were flower children who played the Café Au Go-Go in the West Village. In terms of drugs, the worst we ever hit was acid and grass. The Warhol gang was East Village, very arty, very into heavy drugs and sex. We were scared shitless of those people." But the whole crowd wound up at Max's after their respective gigs, so they knew each other.

Steve Katz took his new production duties seriously. Reflecting on Bob Ezrin's collapse, he decided never to compete with Lou but to use instead his own intelligence and affection for the artist. The approach must have been valid, for he remained Lou's producer through three (actually, almost four) albums during one of the most explosive periods of his career

Admittedly "naive", Steve decided to experiment with Lou's lifestyle. Consulting an imaginary *Compleat Producer,* specifically the chapter entitled "How To Gauge Your Artist's Synapse Sources" he tried speed, and took half a Desoxyn. "For two days, I was shaking so hard I couldn't press the play button on a cassette recorder. After I recovered, I found out that Lou, for the most part, used drugs very wisely. The man really knew his own capacity. He would take pure methamphetamine hydrochloride and grind it down, and include the whole experience in his music. Then after a month or two he'd decide to clean out his system. He'd stop entirely and move on to

health foods and lifting weights. He knew exactly how to gauge the limits of his tolerance.

"The trouble is, coming off the drug makes you very nasty. If I'd get a call from the studio that he was in a rotten mood, I'd know he'd decided to stop. I never interfered with these decisions . . . I just worked around them. I knew when I was speaking to the man, and when I was speaking to the drug. Most of the time he was a considerate, warm human being and a real friend. And I will say, hands down, he was the most brilliant man I have ever known."

Their concept of the live album went through a few changes. "The songs were so powerful they could be interpreted in a number of ways. At first he wanted a real heavy metal style, because the band was so incredible. But as the tour evolved, he went back to the basic Velvets feel of certain songs. He always went through changes, I was beginning to learn, he always considered the options. One night in Toronto we were fooling around and I sang *Sweet Jane* and he was ecstatic. '*That's* how it should always have been done – as a ballad!'"

Anyway, the North American tour wound up in triumph at Howard Stein's Academy of Music on 14th Street on December 21st. Guiding a Record Plant mobile unit, Steve watched a capacity crowd explode into frenzy to a revitalized *Heroin. White Light/White Heat, Rock and Roll* and a distinctly unsentimental version of *Sweet Jane.* Also included was a raunchy *Lady Day,* minus any of the delicacy of *Berlin*'s artful arrangement. A lot of fans still think it was one of the most spectacular concerts of their lifetime. Lou later characterized the performance as "manic".

RCA released the album six weeks after the concert and called it *Rock n Roll Animal* – it had excellent reviews. By the end of March 1974 it had soared to #45, remaining in the hot 100 for 27 weeks. *Rolling Stone* used the occasion to debunk the preachy self-righteousness of the *Berlin* slam. Timothy Ferris praised the "sinister and stunning" performance of *Heroin* with "the atmosphere of a cathedral at black mass." He praised Lou as an artist of "honesty and musical brilliance and courage. He never blinks."

In *Zoo World* Wayne Robins wrote that Lou might look like "a cross between a mad executioner and an overgrown rodent" but he had become, finally, "a rocker and not a chanteuse". Lou appeared amused by the media flap, espeically those delirious reviews wishing that the guys in this band had done that

November 1974 Michael Zagaris

November 1974 Michael Zagaris

David McGough

John Cale, Patti Smith and Lou backstage at the Bottom Line *Chuck Pulin*

Top left: *L.F.I.*
Below left: Nico Steve Katz
Top right: Lou and Nico Steve Katz
Below right: Chuck Hammer

Top left: Lou and his wife Sylvia Morales Barry Schultz RETNA
Below left: Steve Katz
Right: Richard Verdi

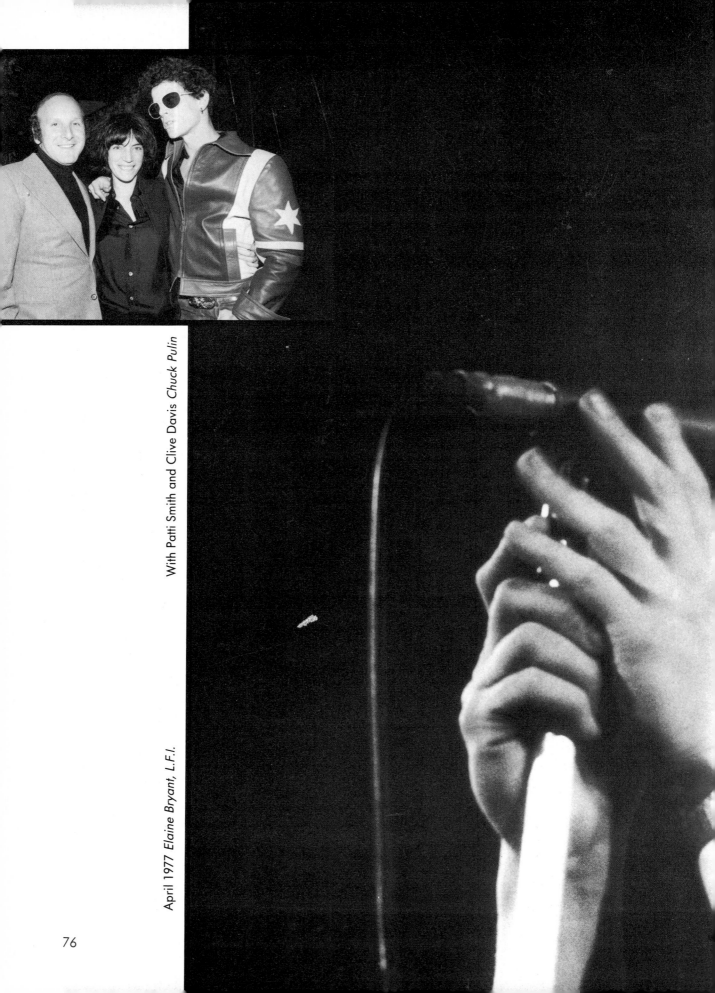

With Patti Smith and Clive Davis *Chuck Pulin*

April 1977 *Elaine Bryant, L.F.I.*

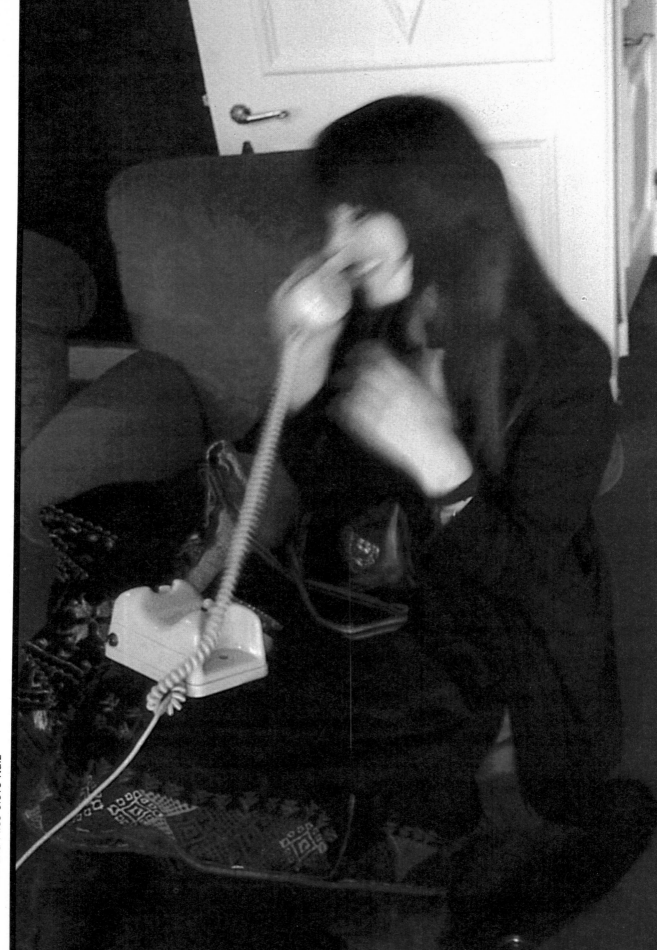

Lou and Nico *Steve Katz*

Mick Rock

Berlin record. Responding to the type of review that declared *Heroin* "thirteen minutes of maddening tease that finally releases you to a frenzied orgasm – a shuddering, bestial come!" he explained coolly that, "We just go out and play some rock and roll. It's what the Velvet Underground was all about . . ."

Steve Katz was very happy with the success of his first production efforts. "I never came to regret the aesthetics of this album – which is more than I can say about others we were involved in. It reflected precisely where Lou was

at the time, with the exact band he wanted, and the specific interpretation of his songs he'd wanted to try for some time."

Rock n Roll Animal still stands as one of the great live recordings. Five years later, Billy Altman rated it "a riveting tour de force", lauding Lou's "chilling vocals". He gave it five stars in *The Rolling Stone Record Guide,* the book's highest rating. But at the same time Lou was calling it a crass, commercial effort he was somehow maneuvered into. "It was like a walking time-warp to me . . . but I had to get

80

popular." He admitted that people love the album and that the musicians, specifically Hunter and Wagner, and John Prakash on bass, were outstanding, but . . .

"Now Lou's erased that whole period," observes Katz. "What he won't mention is that he's gotta take some responsibility for it. He never looks back and says, 'Well – it was what I wanted to do at the time.'"

In Motor City, Lou again met one of the few rock writers he took seriously, Lester Bangs, *Creem* editor and literate loudmouth. Lester's allegiance began in 1968 when the Velvet Underground played San Diego. "Lou Reed is my hero," he explained in *Creem*, "because he stands for all the fucked up things that I could ever possibly conceive of – which probably only shows the limits of my imagination." Very quickly artist and acolyte discovered they approved the same authors, pharmaceuticals and juice – Johnny Walker Black. "The tension between them was incredible," recalls Steve. "And it was a relationship that endured – even with their constant needling and jabbing at one another. I hope Lou realises now how much Lester became part of his life and appreciates him."

Lester's empassioned love of Lou knew no reasonable limits. When writing of other artists, he would gratuitously contrast their deficiencies with *Rock n Roll Animal*.

The affection was lifelong. But being loved by Lester was a mixed blessing. When Lou changed hairstyles, roommates, band members, hair colours, or even guitar straps, Lester was right there to laugh out loud. Now and then, it got on Lou's nerves, but he never made himself inaccessible.

From America, the tour blazed on to Europe. Wife Betty was still with Lou. Her all-American niceness contrasted sharply with the hysterical. rock-savage image Lou projected on stage. It was a happy and balanced time. Nico visited in Paris. The two had not seen each other since their Bataclan performance in '72 with John Cale. She was still entrancing.

Before leaving for the Continent, Lou got in touch with Sterling Morrison in Austin, Texas. After being without a phone for two years, so as to discourage Velvets parasites from seeking him out, Sterling had felt it was safe to be accessible. Wrong. "I started getting these calls from Steve Sesnick, and I thought, what is this bullshit? Then *Lou* even called. Apparently his lawyer had told him to turn on the charm. They wanted me to sign for the release of the 1969 *Velvet Underground Live* album.

"I did *not* want it released . . . You know there is a certain clean feeling that comes from not dealing with the people you'd have to, to collect royalties on anything like that. And I'd listened to the tapes and I thought – oh man! I can't see this selling ten copies. Musically I much preferred *Live at Max's* – it has much more energy. I said I was not going along with it.

"I was told if I continued with this attitude, dragging my feet, then the album wouldn't come out at all. I said I had no need to bolster a sagging career with something like this . . . but fine, I hope you put it out tomorrow so I can start suing you. Then Steve Sesnick finally convinced me. I signed the release for a pittance because he told me he needed the money. I'm sure he was in cahoots with Lou in some strange way. Meanwhile, Mercury had pressed ahead with the production. That's why I wasn't listed anywhere on the record, because I wasn't . . . cooperating."

1969 *Velvet Underground Live* is four sides of live material recorded in Texas and San Francisco in 1969. Although Sterling maintains that "other performances on that tour are ten times better," critic Paul Nelson selected extended versions of *New Age, Sweet Jane* and *What Goes On*. There was a lot of fine, freewheeling guitar work from Sterling, and the increasing organ intensity in *What Goes On*. The best thing about the set is that each song is run out to its allowable, and in the case of *Ocean* beyond, musical limit. The basic structure was so strong that it allowed endless reworking and improvisation. Patti Smith reviewed the album for *Creem* in 1975 shortly before she abandoned her career as a critic, and said she liked it because it was oppressive.

There are two great things about the cover. One is the liner notes from Elliott Murphy which contain the sentence "Rock n roll people tend to live on the edge. (That's what this album is all about.)"; and other comments about how the band "played sad music". Most remarkable is the cover itself, a rear crotch shot of a young nymph in leopard-print bikini and boots of shiny leather, by the great, late Ernie Thormahlen.

In the booklet *Lou Reed – Words and Music*, Lou told Barry Miles that the gentle, sentimental version of *Sweet Jane* recorded here had "the original lyrics – even recorded the day I wrote it . . . the first night we'd ever played it. Some rich kid in Texas had a sort of club . . ."

81

SALLY CAN'T DANCE
LOU REED LIVE

"This is fantastic — the worse I am, the more it sells. If I wasn't on the record at all next time around, it would probably go number one."
Lou *to Danny Fields in Gig*

Sally Can't Dance is one of the most curious offerings of Lou's seventeen-year career. Since denounced by Reed, his co-producer Steve Katz, and even, by extension, his label, which cheerfully let it go out of print, it is for some reason the most popular album he ever made. By the late autumn of 1974, this "crappy concession to commercialism," as Lester called it, had actually gone Top Ten, reducing everyone associated with it to stunned solvency. "If *Sally* is a commercial success," mused *Crawdaddy*, "Lou will have orchestrated the greatest irony of his irony-loving life."

The album is close to autobiography, with injections of relevant biography. The heroine of the title track, who of course OD's, is a onetime top model who used to "ball folksingers" but has shot so much meth she has lost her looks and can't "dance".

Where *Berlin* was ambiguity and nuance, *Sally* is not difficult for the average Reed freak to figure. *Kill Your Sons* is a song about a sensitive youth who has a nervous breakdown not at all helped by his parents' forcing him into electroshock therapy in Freeport, Long Island. The rollicking *New York Stars* is on-going Warholiana. *Billy* is a personality study of two distinct types, one reprobate rock and roller and one med student who gets all A's. Of

course there is the usual savage twist: the med student goes to war and comes back shattered, while the rock and roller turns his obsessive lifestyle into a relatively successful form of expression. Of the two friends, he observes, "No one could figure out which one of us was the fool." To play bass for this mini-parable he brought Doug Yule out of retirement. "He told me, 'You have the right style for this,'" Yule related to Philip Milstein in *What Goes On. Crawdaddy* told him he was "incompetent".

Eight years later, the album's imbalances still disappoint. "Oh, I do regret *Sally Can't Dance*. What a rotten album," confesses Steve Katz. Actually, as coproducer, he took a less-than-bloody lambasting from the press. In the *LA Times,* Robert Hilburn noted that he and Reed had "obviously spent some time listening to *Transformer*", thus making his vocals more accessible on the title track. But their handling of the remaining five "is simply too narrow and conservative to bring out the essence of Reed's material." Studio stalwart Richard Robinson showed an unexpected empathy in *Hit Parader,* calling Katz's production "admirable" and telling Lou, in an open letter, that it's "the closest you've been to being heard for some time." But he regretted *Sally*'s lack of depth, energy and rock and roll craziness, which had him virtually unable to distinguish one song from another.

"I'll take all the blame for this album," Steve insists. But the project was booby-trapped from its inception. Ragged and sleepless, Lou wrote all the songs in the studio in the month of June, except *Kill Your Sons*, which had its lyrical origin during the Velvet years. "As an artist," admits Steve, "Lou was not totally . . . there. He had to be propped up like a baby, with things done for him and around him. Clearly, this was the situation he wanted. The drugs were becoming just too much for me to deal with.

"Later on he started giving out interviews claiming he was 'surrounded by schlock artists' — not so. Sometimes even great artists have no hindsight. Michael Suchorsky, Prakash John, Whitey, Danny Weiss — these were musicians he had used — or would use — for years and years. We all loved and understood him and tried to help him. But he simply refused to be *there.* Most of the time he was in the bathroom shooting up. One time at my home in Westchester he just disappeared, and I was getting fairly fed up, so by 'accident' I opened up the bathroom door. He looked at me looking at the

needle and said, startled, 'Oh — now you know.' I was ready to burst out laughing. *Now* I know?"

During this period Lou was getting his divorce from Betty, the "pretty blonde princess" he had lived with, basically, since 1971. Everyone who has ever spent fifteen minutes with her comments on her sweetness and emotional generosity. "She is so pure . . . and I believe in sparrows . . ." he once rhapsodized to Ed McCormack in *Fusion*. Now he told Lester on the psychotic *Sally* tour that "she was a secretary when one was needed."

He now kept company with the legendary Rachel, far and away one of the most arresting figures in recorded music. Rachel was a tall, beautiful, half-Mexican transsexual supposedly raised in reformatories and prisons since a tender age. "Imagine . . ." recalls Steve, "a woman in a man's body, getting by as a juvenile delinquent. Understanding Rachel was a question of understanding a person's orientation. I found her wonderful, and very quiet. That whole thing about, was Lou homosexual, was he straight — Rachel was physically gorgeous for *any* sex. Straight men were coming on to her all the time."

Lou's sexuality had become extremely important to thousands of fans since the opening note of *Venus in Furs*. Dave Hickey recalled in *Oui* that roadies were constantly being asked if their leader was "bi". "Bi? The fucker's *quad!*" one perhaps retorted — anyway, the *bon mot* bounced around the world. "In my experience," Hickey wrote, "and we spent a lot of time together, all these supposed 'digressions from the norm' were just bullshit. Essentially Lou Reed is a straight-ahead kid from Long Island who graduated from Syracuse University.

"Anyway, if you took that much speed for that many years, you don't know what the hell you are. Physically, you *cannot* get an erection. Whenever he'd start talking about his prowess, I'd know for sure he wasn't getting it up, and therefore going to extremes. Psychologically, I don't think he's definitely oriented one way or another. But he had the brilliance to dip in and out of deviance, and play with it, make an illusion of it.

"But head games were his true life's passion. He had an ability to manipulate other people that is unmatched, at least in my experience. He could not take the responsibility for his life and his mistakes so he spent a lot of time making them the responsibility of other people. He

needed a psychiatrist, and there isn't one in this world that's a match for him.

"The idea was to be always *on*. It was *always* showtime. One night we were at Max's and he ordered a Singapore Sling. He sat there behind his sunglasses and for one hour he did not take a sip. Finally I said, 'Uh . . . Lou . . .' and he said, 'That's just the point. People are watching me. It's very hip to order a drink and never touch it.'

"Yeah, he was on all the time, but he could be objective, and he had a real sense of humour about it. He was careful to observe all the feedback the 'Lou Reed persona' got in the press . . . he read an enormous number of magazines. He knew he was carrying the weight of the image of the Velvet Underground; he knew Lou Reed had to be Lou Reed. If Lou Reed is supposed to take drugs and have a weird sex life . . . well, then . . . it has to be. In a behavioural sense, a human being simply cannot escape that trap, no matter how brilliant he is."

Sally stayed on the charts for 14 weeks. "My God, I could hardly stay awake during that album. They'd make a suggestion and I'd say oh, all right, and do the vocals and leave," he claimed in a later interview. That is, the vocals he could remember. With *Ride, Sally, Ride* he could not summon them up, and Steve had to sing the song into a cassette and send Lou home to learn it. With disasters compounding, Steve's Westchester home burned down before the final mix, which left him badly shaken.

Lou now left for the most controversial tour of his career. Skeletally thin, with peroxided pineapple hair that replaced his former tonsorial statement, an iron cross clipped close to the skull, he cashed in on his raging popularity. He used album musicians, who cranked the *Sally* material into "a sort of heavy metal R&B with off-the-wall psychedelic overtones," wrote David Baemoth in *Phonograph Record*, noting right off that the show was "massively depressing".

But not, apparently, to the thousand or so other fans at the Allen Theater in Cleveland. "He's drawing genuine Bachman-Turner Overdrive types, who yell out requests for *Sweet Jane* like it's a top 10 hit, and light matches for an encore." Critics sighed while rowdies, fried on downs, cheered the inclusion of the word 'Quaaludes', instead of Valiums in *Walk On the Wild Side*.

Heroin was reintroduced to the tour repertory. A few years earlier when a loyalist requested it during the marvellous Max's summer gig, he had snapped, "We don't do that song anymore." In a number of interviews he bemoaned fans who came up to him asserting that the song was so groovy, they had to go out right away and shoot up. But now it was back in the set list, with a particularly hideous twist.

In *Melody Maker* of December 7, 1974, Todd Tolces described a gory Guignol before 5,000 raving fans in San Francisco. Lou "pulled a hypodermic needle out of his boot . . . as the crowd erupted into cheers and calls for, 'Kill, kill!' he tied off with the microphone cord, bringing up his vein. As the writer ran for the gentlemen's toilet, Lou handed the syringe to a howling fan handy-by." This happened ten or twelve times on the American tour, to consistently approving onlookers, some of whom "actually clapped along to the chorus, in testimony to the density of a collective audience," wrote Gary Peterson.

Mutual hostility rose in waves during some shows, despite the efforts of Danny Weiss and his supporters from the band, Rhinocerous. The standard audience expression, according to Janet Macoska in the Cleveland *Commuter,* "was one of stunned boredom . . . hands barely holding up nodding heads . . . and Lou, half the time, had no idea what he was supposed to be singing." But by the time he reached Detroit, then home turf of Lester Bangs, he had once again managed to focus his rage; Lester said the show was great.

As the two settled into their usual hotel-room Punch & Judy put-downs, Lester was amused by the sight of Rachel sitting passively, turning the pages of a book. "It was a grotesque . . . purely strange. If the album *Berlin* was melted down and reshaped in human form, it would be this creature." Curious, but not exactly sexually aroused; he noted her long, rank hair, beard and "tits . . . or something". He pondered the motivations behind this union. "The cat's gay, he's a celeb, he's got lots of money . . ." and could purchase or persuade any type of sexual amusement he desired. There had to be something meaningful going on with Rachel. Moreover, Lou seemed to border on the protective.

Pretty soon, Lou and Lester got down to wrangling over who was the greater poseur, fraud, sham talent, technological knownothing and speed fiend. Lou told Lester he was a washout in terms of correct methamphetamine consumption because he did not know how to compute his own tolerance or metabolic needs. Lester told Lou that he was just

re-cycling "pasteurized decadent" left over from *Transformer* times. About 3:00 AM Lou started to play the new Ron Wood LP . . .

With the on stage syringes and amp cords tightened just above the elbow, and drunken fans and firecrackers and snapping at reporters, the journey was under constant stress. By the time the artist got to a jam-packed Felt Forum at Madison Square Garden he might as well have been on Mars. "At this point," says Steve, "you could stick him anywhere with the band, and he'd play. When you're that stoned it just doesn't make a difference.

"Mick Jagger was in the audience and he really did want to meet Lou. So he went backstage to his dressing room and tried to strike up a conversation. He said politely, 'Have you ever played here before?' Answered Lou, 'How the fuck should I know?'"

The show then moved to Australia and the Far East, where both Lou and the Velvet Underground had been popular for the previous ten years. The Japanese in particular wrote long articles about the imagery collages in his songs.

Lou and Rachel arrived in Australia, in time for the following press conference:

Press: You sing mainly about drugs?
  Lou: Sometimes.
Press: Why do you do this?
  Lou: Because the government is plotting against me.
Press: Because you like taking them?
  Lou: No . . . because I can't carry them when I go through Customs. I'm hoping that someone in the *audience* . . .
Press: Then you were searched by Customs men for drugs!
  Lou: Naw . . . I'm high on life.
Press: But you sing about drugs. You want people to take them?
  Lou: Oh yeah, I want people to take drugs.
Press: And why is that?
  Lou: Because it's better than Monopoly.
Press: It says in this press release that you lie to the press. Is this true?
  Lou: No.
Press: Would you describe yourself as a decadent person?
  Lou: No.
Press: Well then, what?
  Lou: Average.
Press: Is your anti-social posture part of your show-business attitude?

Lou: Anti-social?

Press: Well, you seem very withdrawn. Do you like meeting people?

Lou: Some.

Press: Do you like talking to us?

Lou: I don't know you.

Press: Would it be correct to call your music gutter rock?

Lou: Oh, yeah.

Press: You sing a lot about transvestites and sado-masochism. What is your role in these songs?

Lou: Eh?

Press: To put it bluntly, are you a transvestite or a homosexual?

Lou: Sometimes.

Press: Well, which one?

Lou: I dunno. What's the difference?

Press: Well, you must like some things in life better than others.

Lou: Oh, no.

Press: But then — how do you spend your money?

Lou: On drugs.

Looking back in anger, Lou has supposedly also "erased" any connection with *Lou Reed Live*, the second album taken from the mobile unit recording at the Academy of Music in December 1973. Yet it's a fine record, with the holocaustal Hunter/Wagner highrolling *Waiting for the Man* and an extended guitar duel in *Oh, Jim* that at one point he heralded as "so fantastic, so classic — and the only reason it went on is because I get off on it."

The vocals are for once, good. In *Rolling Stone,* Paul Nelson lauded its "spectacular, even majestic rock and roll" performed through "the best arrangements, sound and musicians that money could buy." He especially cited *Vicious, Satellite of Love* and *Sad Song.* He hoped that the album would put an end to the assortment of Lou Reed jokes making the rounds. "He is still one of a handful of American artists capable of the spiritual home run."

Creem found the album, and its predecessor, *Rock n Roll Animal,* a straight line to "kids who picked up on Lou Reed because he was new and hip", more than vindicating coproducer Katz's contention that there was a vast new audience out there. Fans can appreciate the "more harmonically complex material from *Transformer* and *Berlin,* which fares better on stage than in the studio." *Vicious,* though, came off "like a cross between *Louie, Louie* and the Allman Brothers," so much does heavy metalization reduce even poetic in-jokes to the throbbing basics.

In *Phonograph Record,* Gary Kenton found it "a good technical document" with class-A rockers "playing it straight and fairly tough behind Reed's warblings and yowlings . . . Reed's vocal style is subtle and essentially passive, and not conducive to the live medium."

Lou Reed Live sold well, though not as spectacularly as *Sally Can't Dance.* It made it up to #62 on the US charts by the early summer of '75, and served to keep happy those who had recently "discovered" him as a rocker. It is still cherished as a blast of adrenalin, and a testament to the idea of linking up classically good material with American boogie. After the recording the entire band minus Ray Colcord, the keyboardist, decamped to the more lucrative pastures of Alice Cooperdom. Lou found Alice limited, derivative and foolish, saying in more than one interview that he embodied "the worst and most disgusting aspects of rock 'n roll."

Lou Reed Live stayed on the charts ten weeks, and its relative success achieved Steve Katz's stated production goal of establishing Lou in the consistent commercial mainstream. Whatever artistic value *Sally Can't Dance* may have lacked, it was appreciated by more of his fans than any other of his albums. The two live albums have gone into reissue and continue to sell. *Rock n Roll Animal* is over 600,000 worldwide.

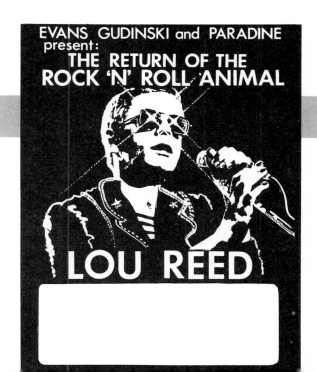

METAL MACHINE MUSIC

"One day in the summer of 1975 I awoke with a hangover and put on Metal Machine Music *immediately. I played it all day and through a party that lasted all that night, in the course of which I got shitfaced again on cognac and beer, broke about half my record collection, punched out the front screen door in my house, physically molested one of my best friends' girlfriend of four or five years, told my friend who was a very talented poet that he couldn't write for shit, after getting thrown out of a restaurant for spilling beer all over his lap and myself and the table and creating a 'disturbance', zoomed over to another friend's house where I physically assaulted her, repeating over and over in a curiously robotlike rant, 'I know you've got a bottle of Desoxyn in your dresser! Gimme, I want them, I want to take all of them at once!,' threw all the empty cognac bottles in the air as high as I could for the pleasure of watching them shatter in the street, ending up in a blackout coma stupor, which nevertheless never blacked me out quite enough to stop me from writhing on the couch, tearing at my hair and screaming at the top of my lungs, until the police came at 7 AM, whereupon I snapped to and told them that my friends, who were now out in the street breaking beer bottles and yelling "MACHINE! MACHINE! MACHINE!" up at my bedroom window, had gotten a little rowdy and I would be responsible for them from here on out."*

Lester Bangs, Concert Review

Metal Machine Music is four sides of shrieking electronic rage directed with technological intensity at a corporate system of supply that would allow *Sally Can't Dance* to go Top Ten. There is more controversy surrounding the conception and promotion of this record than all of the lawsuits the artist has engaged in since the days of the Velvet Underground. But the statements it makes are valid, and have been made by every serious artist in one way or another in response to the hoary question: who am I writing this for, anyway?

On the cover there is Lou lustrous in black leather and the warning, "Combinations and Permutations built upon constant harmonic Density Increase and Melodic Distractions". Inside there is sixty-four minutes and four seconds of white noise drone through alien circuitry. Amongst the frenzied anger and the terrifying drone are occasional and curious 'melodies' that go nowhere. Like *Sister Ray*, wide open at 10, it obliterates all thought, but unlike *Sister Ray* it does not exalt; it just . . . removes.

Everyone loathed *Metal Machine Music* but with disclaimers. Lou loved it with no disclaimers. "On *Sally*, I was imitating me. They really didn't need me around. So I put this out, which didn't *have* me on it, vocally anyway. I decided that would put a stop to it," he stated in *Gig*. It was immediately dubbed *Methedrine Machine Music,* and it certainly had an obsessive amphetamine edge, but the primary drug was distilled rage.

As an electronic signal, it made people stop and think. "Just because it's an amphetamine-head playing around with electronics and tape recorders doesn't mean it isn't valid," Lester cautioned in *Creem*. John Rockwell termed it, "sheer self-destructive indulgence" in the *New York Times*, later remarking that, "if I had bought this album, regardless of store policy of refunds — exchanges only, I would raise hell until I got my money back." In *Rolling Stone*, James Wolcott sniffed, "Lou Reed is disdainfully unveiling the black hole in his personal universe, but the question is, who's supposed to flinch?"

In Japan they love Lou Reed. A Japanese fanzine circulated throughout the Far East had the following review, by Mr. Mibina, of *Metal Machine Music:* "I received a violent shock by this, his greatest album. It is something you can call fearful. The confused electric sound hit me like a long whip and the sound, like a tornado, broke into my head and went around my body

Blakes Hotel, London 1974 *Mick Rock*

David McGough, Retna Ltd

like a wild blood. The sound without weakening the first shocking strength goes on for more than an hour. This album will become something that has never existed in the history of pop music. This is logical music, even though LaMonte Young, who is known as the other composer of experimental music, may be surprised . . .

Amphetamine or ProPhenelyne, which is known with the brand name Benzedrine. This drug is used to recover from tiredness, but you get a habit and side effects: depression, hallucinations and schizophrenia. This reminds me of that."

Other responses ranged from unforgiving fury to disgruntled stupefaction. Ed Ward called it "an act of despicable elitism" and William Howard, in the *Boston Globe* "an appalling rip-off that makes Yoko Ono's wildest put-ons seem artistic by comparison." "This record isn't even a creditable alternative to (his) previous solo offerings, being as it is neither despairingly provocative, oppressive, or anything much . . . it's back to Coney Island, I suppose," sighed Angus MacKinnon in *Melody Maker.*

The artist was having none of this. "I'm not gonna apologize to anybody!" he snapped in a phone interview to *Creem.* "They should be grateful I put that fucking thing out, and if they don't like it, they can go eat ratshit. I make records for *me.*"

In the meantime, poor RCA — "How could his label allow this?" was the current question — decided to cut its losses. They had originally wanted to out it out on the Red Seal classical music label, but then considered Lou's status as a popular and consistently unpredictable pop artist. They could only concur when *Billboard* noted "Suggested cuts — None." They issued an apology to their distributors which the artist immediately repudiated. The thing was not charted in the United States, indication of the corporate disapproval.

After the hue and cry had abated, Lou seemed to remember that he was a commercial recording artist whose future depended on his fans. They might be morons, sex feebs and wimps who used his raw nerves for their own vicarious pleasure, but they bought his records and crowded his concerts. He sent out word through his friend Lisa Robinson's column that *Metal Machine Music* was "ill-timed and misrepresented and I apologize for that." He hoped that his forthcoming album, *Coney Island Baby*, would "make up for any difficulties and disappointments."

Like *Berlin*, the album then began a curious life of its own. Almost immediately out of print, it goes for $50 down at Colony Records. People who recovered from the initial shock sensed, like John Rockwell "a wealth of listenable detail" beneath the primary assault level, and now cherish it in record collections.

"What makes me more confused is the credit on the backside. You see the chemical formula of some drug. The subtitle of this album is The Amine Ring. So I checked and this must be

CONEY ISLAND BABY

"You know . . . that's what Coney Island Baby *is all about. These (critics) . . . they wanted me to OD. And they never even offered me the dope to do it with."*

> *Melody Maker interview*

By the autumn of 1975, Lou was scheduled to go back into the studio to make Coney Island Baby. The new song titles, he announced in *Creem,* were *Dirt, Kicks, Glory of Love, Leave Me Alone, Nowhere At All* and *I Wanna Be Black.* His musical lineup included electric viola, tenor sax, three guitars, drums and bass, "everything that the Velvet Underground was," he announced in Lisa Robinson's column.

RCA was very hopeful. "They said, you can do anything you want so long as it's not *Metal Machine Music,*" he confided. He entered the studio with Steve Katz again slated as co-producer and a full complement of new musicians. Two weeks went by, and some half-finished songs were produced.

This time, Steve found him impossible to work with. Stonewalled by his amphetamine abuse, he quit. "There was no other way. Each day was a new head trip. Finally I said to him, right in front of all the musicians who'd gone through this — 'I give up! If you're gonna play these games, I *know* you're gonna outwit me. I'm just your producer. I acknowledge that you're much smarter than I am — there's no point to playing these games.'

"The drugs had taken over and things were completely crazy. I felt that Lou was, at the time,

out of his mind. So I had to stop the sessions. I had someone in authority from RCA come to the studio and verify that I could not make an album with the artist — that was that."

After some weeks, Lou drew on his ability to clean himself out and bring about a physical resurrection. He pulled back from the abyss and got back into human form. One night at the old Ashley's on lower Fifth Avenue he met Godfrey Diamond, who was to become his new producer. Godfrey, then an engineer at Media Sound in his early 20's "really wasn't a huge fan of his up to this point. I guess I was too young. But I really loved the *Banana* album and *Transformer. Satellite of Love* was a work of art."

After a few rounds, during which the artist discussed his new project, he invited Godfrey back to the Gramercy Park Hotel to hear his tapes and meet Rachel. Godfrey was flattered. "I must say, I thought Rachel was stunning . . . Mexican and gorgeous. But I had the definite feeling . . . they weren't doing well at all. Anyway, Lou plugs in his Telecaster and that into a tape deck and plays me eight new songs that just blew me away. Fortunately, he didn't ask my impression of the last album he'd done — two records of tone oscillation. He never was too clear on where he was coming from with that thing — and believe me, I wasn't asking any questions.

"Another clever thing he did — he never played me the material for the album that was already worked up. I guess he didn't want to jeopardize my head, going into the studio. I really don't know what went on with the original production, but in my case, he turned out to be one of the most cooperative artists I've worked with. Sometimes in the studio, it turns out to be just a clash of personalities . . ."

In asking Godfrey to be his producer, Lou wasn't risking much. An all-around sound technician with solid experience since his teens, Godfrey was also a musician who wrote songs. Lou also knew his brother Jack from the days at the Factory. Mostly, it seemed to be Godfrey's personality which grabbed him. Soft-spoken, nonjudgmental, ambitious, humorous, Godfrey took his production duties so seriously that he twice worked to the point of nervous exhaustion. "I consider the job of producer to mean doing anything that's required to get the sound on the record. The point is to present the artist as brilliantly as possible. You've got to want to get along with him. With Lou that was no problem. You've got to be smart enough

and intuitive enough to see what will make him react. Of course playing any kind of emotional game with Lou is impossible, he's way ahead of anyone . . .

"A good producer fills up all the leaks in the house. He brings up the mood, he fleshes out all the parts . . . provides what it takes. Don't waste time fighting with the artist. Most of the time it just means being cool. Other times it's pushing issues you really believe in. With Lou, the thing I wanted to avoid at all costs was over-production.

"We started out with *Charley's Girl*. He came into the studio with no amp and I put him in an isolation booth with a mike on the guitar, and the amplifiers outside, I fooled him. The song sounded somewhat acoustic but it wasn't, it was fully amplified. What I'm proudest of on that record is that I made it right so he could play. Do you know how long it had been since he'd played on a record? Everyone says how great it is that he was 'speaking like a poet' again. I think it's great that he was relaxed enough to be that tender. How many times have you ever heard Lou Reed get down, like at the very end where he says, 'I swear to God I'd give it all up for you?' How many albums has he done where he's put his heart out like that? The point for a producer is to create a space where an artist can feel free to do that.

"When we were together in the studio he let me handle the board. But one time we were finishing mixing and talking about the fact that we had brought the album in way under budget . . . perhaps we used only 2/3 of the money . . . as I recall; the company gave us a very nice bonus for that. Anyway I was five mixes in and my confidence was really growing. Lou sat down at the board. So I just slipped out of the room and left the assistant there to play back the tapes and let him go wild. I went out and talked to Rachel.

"I always got off talking to Rachel . . . she/he was so amazing. She would talk to my girlfriend for hours about nail polish and style. I must say, hands down, that she is the best haircutter I've ever met. She cut my hair twice and it was gorgeous. And if she is doing anything else with her life at the moment, that's a big mistake. The way they got along . . . she was always there. Then out on the street, Rachel would walk about four yards in front of us, as if to act as Lou's bodyguard . . .

"There was Lou at the board, so happy. Whatever went on with *Metal Machine Music*, I'm here to tell ya the man is not a nitwit — he really digs electronics and he really *knows* electronics. Plus he has a very good ear — he knows exactly what he's hearing. It's not just the fact that he has a tremendous love of playing with equipment. On the album mixes, he would support my work down the line.

"I came back in an hour. Lou was still very happy. I feel it's important for an artist to play with his record, especially when we still have plenty of bread in the budget. Fine. But then I came back in another hour. He was still having a great time. I went out and asked Rachel, 'How long can this go on? Things have been going so well — do you think they might turn weird?' Rachel was very quiet. 'I don't know.'

"I gave the whole thing over three hours. Then I sauntered back in and said, 'Oh Lou — that sounds really great!' Which actually it did. 'Listen to this wall of sound effect!' he yelled. 'I said, 'Great, I can get that, no problem.' With that, he got up and went to his own seat. I went to the board and gave him just that strong a sound on that particular instrument.

"Since then, I've got to say I've known artists with such egos they feel they *must* mess with the producer's head. They love to throw around technical terminology but it adds up to nothing. Unlike Lou, they really do know nothing. But any respectable producer or engineer will just let it ride. He won't say, 'that's not a harmonizer, you're wrong.' A good producer is secure with his own abilities and he takes this board fascination in his stride. The real point is that a competent artist must make it clear to his producer what it is he wants. The producer must know that sure, there's a lot of ego in there, but he must keep an open head, and listen good, and make it into something.

"I'm not saying that due to my brilliant concept of production the whole thing was love and roses. No. I just don't believe that fighting is the best way to get anything out of anyone. We had a few days of sarcastic knocks back and forth. He'd knock Philadelphia and I'd come right back and slam Brooklyn. Sometimes he'd knock my style a little. 'Godfrey is so wonderfully *malleable*,' he announced one night. He wanted to make the point that only he knew what the word meant. I let him go on for a while. I knew he really wanted me to react, but I wouldn't give him the satisfaction. Finally after a while I whispered, a flexible producer accomplishes a lot more.' He dropped it.

"Lou Reed never likes to be wrong. In my production experience, I haven't met anyone who liked to be wrong! One thing that really

Godfrey Diamond, producer of 'Coney Island Baby'

impressed me is that you simply can't put anything over on him. He's always fully aware. I thought he was a real warrior, with such *courage*. He always goes for the tough edge, the risky stuff.

"This doesn't mean he's always a sweetheart to live with. Nobody is, that really knows what he wants. I could see on *Crazy Feeling* that all the antagonism about *Metal Machine Music* was beginning to come out. He was mad at everyone. But that intensity was good. I just decided to pretend all those bad things never happened. We did have something of a discussion on *Street Hassle* and *I Wanna Be Black*. I felt both were excellent, but they did not belong on this album. I thought at this point in his career, the idea was to get the most commercial product possible but without selling out his real fans. To make it playable on both WNEW and (the old) WABC (FM and AM New York radio). *Street Hassle* was brilliant, but it wasn't hooky and it was far too heavy. I couldn't let him slip back into that weird tone head. I had to give him another *Walk On the Wild Side*.

"We cut *Leave Me Alone* which went on another album, the *Best of Lou Reed* compilation. He wanted that thing fierce. 'Gimme a big wall of big guitar sound!' He thought of the upright bass on *Charley's Girl*. The singles that were released were *Crazy Feeling* and *Charley's Girl* . . . that last one could have done better; I personally was always crazy about the title song and *My Best Friend* and *Kicks*.

"Lou and I collaborated on everything. At one point he asked me to do the background vocals with him. I said, 'I can't sing but if that's what you want.' I got up and let the assistant run the

board. In terms of a working relationship, I wasn't trying to make points. I'd just be upfront: 'Say, why don't you go out there and get a little tender at this point?' Or, 'this needs background fill — what do you think?'

"Anyway, we came to the end of the album right on schedule, no loose ends. I really didn't have that much going on. I started to get into the R&B and disco stuff I'd be involved with for a while. But Lou called and said, 'Look, there's this old friend of mine from school out in San Francisco. I promised I'd get him a record deal. And you've got to help me produce the album.' What the hell, I was dying to produce. So we went into rehearsal. The material was weird, but a few songs had potential, especially *Wild Angel.* Lou had Mick Rock — he loved his work, we both do — do the cover, just like *Coney Island Baby.* I had him do all my covers after that.

"I finished up Nelson and went on a cruise with my girlfriend, who kept a boat down in Barbados. Then I got a call in Nassau — Lou's back in the studio, remixing! He patched a call through to me by way of my girlfriend's father's company. He's in the studio, he doesn't care if he has to work with the maintenance man, and why don't I come right back? I said no, that mix is fine, it sounds great. Sure enough when I get back, two cuts have been remixed. When he's alone in the studio he goes wild at the board. But he knows his stuff. Me, he was unhappy with, for a time. But he did call me up and ask me to produce two more of his albums.

"Just then he asked me to go on the road with him, to work on the sound, choreograph the show, and so on. But I had to stay in the city, where the production jobs were.

"Because of this, I was starting to get known a little. I met Lester Bangs for the first time. We had dinner to discuss the record. I loved that man. I have a crazy schedule, and his was the only call I'd take at 10 in the morning after being in the studio all night. When he called me at first I thought he was just some madman out in Detroit. Lou introduced us when he was considering touring with Bowie right after *Coney Island Baby.* Before he kicked, we kept in regular touch, we'd call each other.

"Danny Fields . . . he's a very close friend of Lou's. Now the instant the album is finished, we went down to his apartment in the Village. It was very important that Lou heard what Danny thought first. We put on the cassette, it hadn't even been pressed yet. This is my first job as a full producer and I am incredibly nervous.

Danny has a huge living room, but I slunk over and sat in the far corner. Danny sat in a chair very close to the speakers. When I got the nerve to look up – there he was, reading a newspaper! Holding it in front of his face – with Lou right in front of him! I thought that was incredibly rude. Lou whispered, 'See, he does that so you can't see his face.' He thought that was really cool. As I said, I was very new to this critic stuff.

"Danny scribbled down a few notes as he was listening. At the very end he put down the newspaper and announced that he *loved* it. 'Great! – Not one bad song!' He said something about it being as good as his stuff with the Velvet Underground. Then I started breathing again. Before that, I was starting to choke. We stayed there till 8 or 9 in the morning. I had to be at work in a few hours, but I didn't care. Danny had played this cassette for us of this band nobody ever heard of – new wavers called the Ramones. He said he was their manager and wanted to get them a deal. But who the hell were they?

"When he put on the cassette, Lou and I loved them! 1-2-3-4 – really up stuff! I hadn't heard that kind of energy in a long time. We both knew they were going to happen. So Lou and I looked at each other and said, 'Let's do it – get 'em signed, then produce 'em.' Danny was just a little bit unsure, because they weren't yet a proven entity.

"We went around to all the major labels and they wouldn't even consider it. 'You call this rock and roll – this fast shit? We're in a disco phase, a ballady black trip.' We'd answer, 'But what about the future? Maybe the day will come when people want to dance to this kind of rock and roll.

"But their minds were closed. We'd been to seven majors, and we gave up. With perseverence and a tremendous amount of faith, Danny did get them signed, of course.

"So Lou goes out on the road and I go back in the studio. I was at the Record Plant, in Studio B, workin' on Barry Manilow, and I get a hot message from the switchboard – we're 65 with a bullet in *Billboard!* Just imagine that kind of success – coming after a record like *Metal Machine Music.* The first record I'd ever produced, and it actually went top twenty? And sat in there for a *lot* of weeks. Even now, I run into people who are really impressed that I did *Coney Island Baby* . . .

I was really sorry I couldn't work with him on the other two albums. With one, I was so ex-

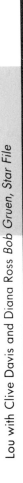

Lou with Clive Davis and Diana Ross *Bob Gruen, Star File*

hausted that I had to stay out of the studio for eight months. I wanted to do an entirely different thing with him. Now I'd take him to Studio A, not B, and open him up to a much bigger sound. Then, I was into tight drums, tight R&B, no ambiance.

"I am so grateful to Lou Reed. I was just a kid, completely unheard of, and he took a chance on me. Together, there were so many things

going against us.

"You know Lou's always wanted Frank Sinatra to sing his work. Two years later I actually did work with Sinatra – I knew a man named Joe Beck, who did arrangements for him. My big dream is to do them together."

"SHE'S MY BEST FRIEND":

THREE YEARS ON THE ROAD WITH TOUR MANAGER BARBARA FULK

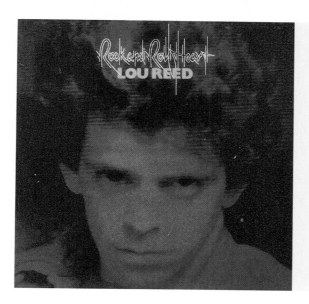

"Lou and I never spent Christmas Eve together, unless he was in jail." Barbara Fulk

"When I first met Lou Reed I was a secretary at RCA Records to the Vice President of A&R, Dennis Katz, who had signed Lou to the label. Previous to this I had no knowledge of the music industry — I'd never even heard of the man. Then I saw him perform at Alice Tulley Hall, his first solo performance in New York. It was incredible! I became a total fan. When Dennis later became part of his management, a tour manager was needed. Ernie Thormalen had managed the first solo tour and would be with us on and off the whole time I was with Lou. But the New York office definitely wanted a representative on the road.

"The summer before he recorded *Transformer* in 1972, we went all over America. Oh, was that work! Lou wasn't yet that popular except on the coasts, so there really wasn't a lot of money, and of course everyone was disgruntled about that. I did well because I didn't know any better. Lou required a lot of attention, which I was happy to give. But I'd never been on a tour, much less managed one, so I felt I had to do everything. I did all the bookkeeping, plus book all the hotels and make travel arrangements — I didn't know you could get travel agents to do this.

"The important thing to Lou was to have someone around he could trust. He knew me, and he was very close, emotionally, to the people I worked for, so it was a kind of family situation. We had some very jolly times. I got skinny very fast — I'll never have thighs like that again — because I worked so hard. After the studio in London we did a European tour, and the hassles really started. We had had a young band, the poor Tots from Yonkers, and they were let go mid-tour. Then we had Moogy Klingman — the worst. Lou made me be nice to him until he found out he was a jerk.

"Europe was a challenge a minute. I loved working there, but the bookkeeping drove me crazy. German currency one day, then French, then Italian. I had to figure out how much U.S. currency to carry, and how much local, for the *per diem*. Then, I'd have to convert the whole mess back into U.S. currency for my road report.

"Going through Customs with Lou Reed is a wild experience, always. Years after the first tours, I can remember walking him through immigration some place in Italy and he was sound asleep behind his sunglasses. This was in 1975 and we'd just gone through the terrible riots there. We didn't really have drugs — I carried whatever small pieces of pot, or whatever. The band was clean, and I threatened them terribly — I really put the fear of God in them about drugs. Europe of course is famous for easy prescriptions, so Lou would go to a different speed doctor in every country. He truly believed in it! He was forever proselytizing, trying to get me to take some. On tour he'd actually go to medical bookstores, he'd literally carry around written justification for amphetamine! Not only that, but he knew how to pronounce it correctly, in every language.

"Lou was not stupid. But with all his knowledge, he could not realise that he was not immune from the effects of the drug. It became a whole vicious cycle. The syringes he used in that 'act' onstage were so easy to get. On tour everyone gets sick, and it was my job to inject band members and roadies with penicillin and so on. European drugstores give you syringes instead of pill prescriptions. But the stage thing was a show. He never really shot up. Just wrapped the damn mike chord around his arm, and thought he was putting something over on everyone.

"Of course I had no personal life. I threw myself into being totally devoted to Lou; he was my whole *raison d'être*. Things were tight, and we were always short of money. On our first tour — I believe Garland Jeffreys opened for us — it was all colleges and rental cars. The next year, 1973, a very tender Hall and Oates opened for us. That same year Lou got some sort of publishing deal and there was more of a cash flow. But never a real profit. I was, at times, a real jerk. I'd pay the roadies before I'd pay myself because God forbid they should quit. And the money had to be managed. Lou didn't handle his own finances because, to put it mildly, he wasn't oriented towards that.

"All of his expenses were taken care of. But one of the things Lou loves best is shopping. If he thought perhaps he should have a larger allowance, or he was in a bad mood, he'd charge things up at the hotel. But he could learn. I trained him to save receipts. He'd come up to me with his pockets full of funny pieces of paper for cigarettes.

"Lou had very strong habits that of course his fans knew about. On our first trip to Australia, in 1974, I was with Ernie, and his fans would always sneak up to the hotel and give pills to their hero. We had to sleep sometime. We couldn't watch him every minute. This time he ended up with a huge pile of amphetamine pills. So Ernie and I staged a mock 'room robbery'. We called up the front desk and acted horrified – Lou's room had been robbed! Of course we'd just grabbed all the pills and thrown them away. Australia was quite a strain by itself. The moment we came off the plane they had a giant press conference waiting for us, after a ghastly 30-hour flight!

"Besides this, this man could drink. When we first got together we had some trouble because his wife Betty was also on the road with us. You can imagine – when you have a female road manager on tour whose job it is to be the artist-looker-after, the wife does *not* like this. She did try and help him. For a while she got him off speed. But the two of them really liked to drink, so keeping them sober was a real exercise in tap dancing. All our tour riders stipulated the Johnny Walker Black in the dressing room.

"I would give him a big belt just before he went onstage. But I knew that if I ever let him anywhere near a full bottle, he'd just drink it all. I once saw him consume fifteen straight tequilas – doubles! – in a drinking contest with a drummer in New Zealand. And then he *walked* away.

"At our hotels his room service trays would be cluttered with glasses. But the really amazing thing was his control. No matter how he carried on, he would always go onstage exactly the same. Sometimes I had to carry him to the stage. Sometimes he'd be out binging for three days and he'd be so exhausted I'd have to put

ice down his back to get him awake enough to carry out to the limousine. Once at the gig, he'd fall sound asleep in the dressing room. But when I said, 'Lou, it's time to go on', and carried him to the stage, the moment he went on he'd appear fully awake, aware and ready. His stage presence was absolutely consistent.

"He didn't give a damn what people thought offstage. And people would wonder – who is that mysterious lady who carries him around? Thinking about this, I feel that women make the best road managers. They are caring, they are very strong, and they pay close attention to detail.

"Even his wife, Betty, for all her vulnerability, turned out to be one tough lady. They were married by the time I became tour manager. I will always remember one drive with them late at night, with the two of them snuggling and kissing in the back of a dark car. Now, after their divorce, she's remarried and has a baby. She can't believe she was ever with him. But you do what is called for at the time.

"Lou requires a lot of care and attention, which I was happy to give to him. But as a woman on the road, I found myself becoming twice as bitchy and forceful with promoters and concert people as I'd ever imagined I would be. I had to, or they wouldn't take me seriously. They assumed I was a groupie, or at best, a secretary. I had to demand all our rights at the box office. In certain places where Lou wasn't doing all that well and was still an obscure cult figure, I had to fight tooth and nail for every little perk rightfully due. We were doing basically theatres, and would perhaps go into percentages five times on an entire tour.

"He was always very big, of course, in New York, New Jersey, Los Angeles and parts of the midwest. I remember the promoter giving me a big kiss in Ohio, because Lou always sold out. But other promoters would pull endless stunts. One wanted to add a third act, and I'd have to make a scene. Lou couldn't stand anyone on stage and so I was constantly heaving people out of the wings. Oh, they would call me terrible names.

"As to my attitude towards myself, I was one of the guys, on one hand, and everyone's mom, on the other. I was the Lou-looker-after, and very, very protective of him. No matter how many stories you hear about his nastiness, whatever, he was very vulnerable. If I had no social life or female friends, I really didn't miss them. We were moving so fast it was a total energy drain. It was very strong physical and

March 1978 at the Old Waldorf, San Francisco *Michael Zagaris*

mental and emotional work. If something went wrong in the middle of nowhere, I had to figure out how to make it right. I had to keep Lou on an even keel at all costs — I was in all aspects his personal attendant. But I enjoyed it. I dealt with the record companies, the press and the promoters, the hotels and the sound companies. I liked having to be resourceful on a moment's notice. I liked having the buck stop at my head. And it kept the juices jumping.

"My all time tour coup was when our bass player — was this in '74? — had his passport stolen. He had no ID. It was all gone. I got him a new passport in Brussels, Belgium on a Sunday. I roused a photographer to come take a picture of him in the hotel lobby, and of course I was carrying his work permit. After that they all thought I was wonderful. After that, also, no one carried his passport.

"I won't pretend it was all one hilarious party. But Lou and I did get along surprisingly well. I knew where my strengths lay, and how to provide the things Lou would look to me for. And I do remember some incredible moments — many incredible moments. On the *Transformer* tour, a mutual friend introduced me to Julie Christie when she was doing *Uncle Vanya* in London. Backstage, she had a copy of *Transformer* on her dressing table. Later, I took her to one of the *Berlin* recording sessions in London. When she heard the music she cried. Everyone adored her. Bob Ezrin, among others, had a terrible crush on her. Ezrin was a true romantic and a wonderful buddy. But this album was becoming a grand passion with him, a way of life. I'll never forget him calling me up from the hospital after his wife had to put him away. He was delirious — but not for long.

"Anyway, Julie started coming to our gigs in Britain and hanging out at the hotel. She'd even travel on the bus with the band. We all became inseparable friends. Back in New York we decided to go see Peter Allen at Reno Sweeney's with Lou and his friend Barbara Hodes. There were eight of us. Lou really liked Julie. He really liked all of us. But he would not stop talking through the entire performance. Offstage, Peter said to Ernie Thormahlen, 'I'm going home to burn my copy of *Berlin*!'

"Other stars admired him greatly. He never came out and said it, but I think he was touched when they found him pretty nifty. I'll never forget Mick Jagger crouching down behind the amps at the Felt Forum so he didn't detract from Lou's performance. I would bring him little glasses of champagne. Mick wanted to come right back into the dressing room and tell him how fabulous he was. But the truth is, the man would be literally shaking after every performance, it so moved him. He'd be wringing wet and he'd need to cool down. But he looked up to Dennis tremendously, and Dennis would bring people backstage, and Lou couldn't refuse him anything. But he couldn't take that much heavy attention all the time. Often the record company would want to take him out to dinner before a tour date. Often Lou did not want to go, so I'd drag all the roadies for a free meal. And he really was very democratic — he'd insist we all stay in the same hotel and be a sort of family. There were many times when Lou and I would say, 'I honestly don't feel like looking at you today' and stay in our separate rooms. But there was a real camaraderie. Travelling together, you live very closely with someone, especially when you're washing his socks, packing his suitcase, and throwing ice down his back so he'll wake up enough to get dressed.

"Some things were just . . . beyond hilarious. He was arrested in Miami on the *Transformer* tour while he was onstage singing *Sister Ray* and making suggestive gestures. There was a fierce line of helmeted policemen directly in front of the stage. Lou would playfully beat them on the head with the microphone as he was crooning *Sucking on my Ding-Dong*. They took him away. I'll never forget that one big policeman standing there with his hand on Lou's shoulder saying, 'This man is going to jail.' Lou thought that was very funny.

"Europe the next year became particularly exhausting. Even with the riots and tear gas in Italy, Lou was always trying to find speed. I had to wash the tear gas out of the roadies' eyes and take them to the hospital. These riots had nothing to do with Lou; they just chose our arena as their battle site, because there were so many people there. The Fascists and the Communists were trying to influence elections, so they threw tear gas at the stage. Why? The riot police were all over the place with big shields.

"And so I cancelled Bologna and took him to a neutral country, Switzerland. He was so upset that he demanded that part of the New York management team come over right away. Plus Tony DeFries, poor man, who was in New York at the time. When Tony arrived off the plane, Lou was so chagrined he didn't want to see him anymore. After *Transformer,* three years later, they were still talking about Tony's someday managing him. Lou could not resist flirting with the idea. But now he holed up tight in a hotel room in Zurich and would not come down. I guess he couldn't face him. Tony and I had coffee together and he got back on the plane.

"Things were starting to go sour. Lou was having convulsions from the speed. Fortunately a member of his family was around to help me. I can remember shoving Valiums down him. Like all drug freaks, he felt he had complete control over the drug. In my experience, no matter how intelligent or visionary a person might be in the other parts of his life, no matter how intimate his knowledge of the drug's effects, he still thinks he's stronger. And Lou had a much larger ego than your average speed freak.

"This could make him quite a comedian. One time in Japan he was sitting with the nicest man from RCA, telling him precisely why they lost the war. Also demanding that he produce a videotape recorder this very moment, or he was going home. Lou always had to have a new gizmo. Then he'd leave them in hotel rooms, and I'd be trailing after him, gathering up his toys.

"Every day kind of invented itself. In a couple of tours in England, it was just Lou and me in a Daimler, with our driver. The band would be behind us in a bus. Every morning I'd go buy his Marlboro cigarettes and some sandwiches and soda and we'd take off.

"One of my favourite stories is about Nico, who would often visit us on tour. One time in New York, Lou decided he wanted to see her and invited her to come over from Paris. She arrived. Once the whim passed, Lou kicked her out — and I had to put her up in my apartment. Of course no one thought to spring for a hotel. I'll never forget coming home to find her on my doorstep, sitting with her harmonium and her candles.

"By the end of 1974, he was becoming more erratic. Dennis suggested that he go to his own doctor. Lou looked up to him so much that he trotted off. I can't imagine his doing this for anyone else. The doctor reported that Lou had . . . slightly elevated cholestrol. Ha! Lou never let Dennis forget this. His idea of a real doctor, of course, was the notorious Dr. Feelgood. Sometimes he'd be waiting on the Doctor's steps at 6 AM.

"Speed is insidious, and the personality changes are radical. Lou would go from being a nice Jewish boy from Long Island to a paranoid maniac. He would have hallucinations about intricate Machiavellian plots working against him. That's why he was always suing — when in doubt, litigate. Other occasions merited more violence. He took his reviews very seriously and sometimes wanted to kill the writers, no matter how much they adored him. The instant you slow down the stroking, he wants to know why. He assumes it's always for the worst reasons.

"He became steadily more volatile. I won't say there wasn't provocation, from time to time. In 1975, his management hired a man named Alec to be tour manager, so I could work back in the office. His qualifications were that he used to be an antique Maserati mechanic. In no time Lou hated Alec so much, he was smashing coke bottles and putting the broken shards of glass in his pocket. He was going to get him. He wound up cutting his hand. Another time he became furious at a tour car — the car. He started beating it up. The RCA reps were speechless. People would say to me, 'How could I stand this behaviour?' But we were under a lot of pressure.

"The game never ended. On Christmas Eve once, in the middle of Long Island, I had to scrape up $500 of my own money to get him out of jail — some misunderstanding about a 'scrip for guess-what. I got our driver and the white Cadillac limo and waltzed out to Riverhead in my best bib and tucker. I remember being amused but thinking, 'This is beginning to get heavy.' He seemed to be diving into the whole nefarious world of drugs.

"Our last tour of Australia is what did it. I was exhausted — this was mid '75, and we'd been pushing very hard, all over the US and Europe, behind *Sally Can't Dance*. Lou had become involved with Rachel but it was too late for Rachel to get a visa. Lou got on the plane. Once in Australia he called Rachel constantly. One time he fell asleep over the receiver. After some time the hotel operator called my room. I told her to just disconnect.

"The separation made him so sad he became emotionally overwrought. My routine of being the bookkeeper, the bouncer, and big mama really wasn't covering the gaps. It all really started with *Metal Machine Music*, an album I didn't particularly like. I didn't tell him this, but I didn't praise it to the skies, either. Before this I was his biggest fan and strongest support, always convincing him he was the cult musical figure of the century to be cherished and protected.

"But as I said, the instant the stroking

stopped ... and he noticed instantly that I wasn't carrying around reviews of the album and passing them out to strangers on the street. He got progressively more nasty. It was awful at the end, and I had to abstain, and just leave. I got on a plane and got out of Australia. I was very upset. I stopped for a while in Tahiti because I changed planes there. As I walked down the ramp, I realised I hadn't taken a vacation in seven years.

"When I got to LA, all the stories about Australia came flooding to me. They were the usual paranoia — but still sad. One person we'd worked with said, 'You know, he's telling people you ran off with some of the receipts.' I said, 'Are you kidding? He owes me $1,300 in back salary!' Seven years later, he *still* owes me $1,300 in back salary.

"Later on, we got drunk together and had a big discussion about all this at Ashley's. He had worked out amazing, intricate plots. I told him it all was a totally open book. All the information was common knowledge, accessible to anyone. He seemed very reasonable about it, at the time."

107

Lisa Robinson: So what do you think Arista will do for you that RCA didn't?
Lou: Sell records.

Interview in Hit Parader

In mid 1976 Lou left RCA with swapped lawsuits and moved to Clive Davis' young Arista label. The vibe apparent was that Clive was a turntable tycoon sensitive to the plight of the misunderstood cult artist. Lou was seen in a number of magazines with his arm around Patti Smith, whose working knowledge of dead symbolists, leather bravado and rhythmic rebellion approached his own, although more noisily. Patti was also on Artista and had made an excellent album with John Cale, *Horses,* that was not about to make Barbra Streisand tremble in her baby-python boots.

On Arista Lou turned out six intensely personal, uneven and somewhat experimental albums, although none even nodded at the *Metal Machine Musings.* The most remarkable of these is the excellent *Street Hassle*, originally slated to be produced by Godfrey Diamond (according to him) and then awarded to Richard Robinson, whose production work almost everyone initially lambasted on the first solo album and then came to appreciate for its clarity and charm.

Street Hassle is his only solo work apart from *Berlin* to return to the street narrative which initially set him apart as a declamatory poet with a band. In an insinuating whisky-roughened voice, he leads with, "Its been a long time since I've spoken with you," and then delivers the real goods, as clean and direct as Robinson's original production six years earlier. The album details Reed's feelings on the evolution of *Rock n Roll Animal* which channelled his rage and disappointment into statements immediately accessible. He is still the fugitive in rebellion against the emotional cost of existing on this planet, and he is not mellowing, not acquiesing, even in the name of self protection: "some people/they just don't know when to stop . . ."

The title track caused critics to pronounce this album his finest solo work. Eleven minutes long, its simple, traditional melody is burned in through hypnotic repetition, first with a Cale-esque cello ("with Cale on, you could focus in on that one string," he told Billy Altman in *Creem*) and moving into guitar and bass. *Street Hassle* is about love seized and the various possibilities open to us, enjoyed and then torn away by access, by the overdose. The three Reed stories are Lou at his most evocative. In the classic poetic tradition he calls up emotion — in this case the tragedy of love — by fleeting, suggestive descriptions of what actually went on. The emptiness of aftermath has always been his special province: "there's nothing left to say".

Bruce Springsteen, recording downstairs at the record plant during Lou's occupation, was called in for a vocal cameo, a particularly sensitive scrap of poetry. "I'm too much of a smart ass," Lou told Billy Altman again, "and I knew he'd do it seriously, 'cause he really is of the street." Maybe he felt that the open tenderness of *Coney Island Baby* album had verged dangerously near the sentimental, a gangster/prankster mood, but the pain of the emotion can never be denied, never allowed just to . . . slip away.

Lou was on Arista only a year when he made his third grand tour of the Far East, beginning with Australia, where he had a large following. Bruce Kirkland, now President of Stiff, USA, was then a young general tour manager for Evans, Gudinski Bookings in Melbourne, hyping a high-profit return for the *Rock n Roll Animal.*

Kirkland remembers that there was "a lot of resistance to the plan. Many promoters said that because of his background and his so-called wild reputation as a drug fiend, and the fact that he might not do interviews, and even the possibility that he might not show up, although having been paid advance money – we would have to think about this. In truth it was all hearsay. No one had ever suffered first hand. But they would.

"Everywhere he was booked sold out straightaway. The flight arrangements were completed. But Lou did not get on the plane in New York. He would not leave without Rachel. Of course we were desperate, and agreed to this. Sussing him out, this was all part of his carefully calculated 'game' process. He knows just how to use a situation in his maneuvering techniques.

"He seemed to believe it was necessary to do something strong right at the start of the tour relationship, to establish his *modus operandi*. Once he had secured his love Rachel, I must say he was cooperation itself, very cool.

"He gave us an interview when he arrived in

Melbourne which went on our national TV show, Night Moves. The tour dates were flashed on the screen afterwards. He sold out everywhere – the vibe was there. There is a bit of a cultural lag in Australia. They do not have access to the main media – but they do have the desire and rock TV is very popular. Videos sold a great many albums without the expense of a tour to establish an artist.

"Things were going very well. Lou had brought along a stunning backup singer, also from Brooklyn I believe, Jo Anna Alvernes. She was very well received, even though we had no idea she was coming. She did backup vocals and a few songs of her own. It would seem as if Lou did an efffortless set, but his audiences were always aroused. He had the ability to manipulate his audience totally, with every song in his repertoire at the edge of his fingertips. He would select them to play the mood of

At the New York Academy of Music, 14th Street Chuck Pulin

each separate audience. He played theatres of two to three thousand people, and Australia was a guaranteed place for him to make money.

"The only incident that occurred was when the local record company promotion man in Christchurch had clearly been screwing around all day. Lou was very cool – didn't say a word. Then, precisely before he was due to go on before a sold-out house, he said he would not do the show unless this man was fired.

"He knew exactly who was to do what, and who was letting him down. On an earlier tour he had befriended Ron Blackmore, who had worked very hard to smoothe over any difficulties. Now, as I remember, Lou requested that they travel together again. Ron owns a sound and lighting company that was used.

"Once back in Melbourne, he sensed something amiss. He requested a psychic, and we dug one up. Do not get on an airplane for seven days, said the psychic. He would not budge. For seven days he hung out, got a little sun, did a lot of shopping and had a great time.

"My suspicions were confirmed at the end of our tour, when I saw him go through the same establishing procedure with the next set of booking agents. Let them know who's calling the shots. Then, once satisfied, he'd be fine. He even gave us a press conference where he was quite witty and charming, and a number of press interviews. But I wondered why he went through all that aggravation first?

"Obviously, it was a clever game. He knew we needed him. If he gave us some trouble, day after day, chances are there would come a point where any promoter would say, 'Enough – screw you.' But if he makes his master stroke at the start, it's smooth sailing. If he's happy, I guess it's worth it."

GROWING UP IN PUBLIC

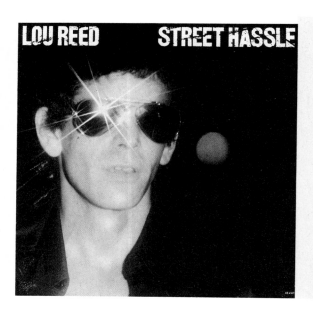

"I simply promised him I was the best Lou Reed guitarist in America."
Chuck Hammer

Chuck Hammer is a guitar prodigy who grew up in the palatial California principality of Santa Barbara. By the age of 24 he felt he had mastered the guitar to the point where he could approach his hero and make application as an acolyte. He wrote Lou a letter. Lou gave him a call. This is Chuck's experience of Lou:

"I told him I was what he needed and he seemed interested. After a while I asked, 'Does anyone in your band know who you are?' 'Not really,' he said. I said, 'I do. You are a genius. *Berlin* is a masterpiece, and I know the music.' That's when I got hired. I could sense from his records that most of his musicians had never listened to him, or if they'd tried, they had no real idea what he was about.

"As a guitarist, coming out of the '70's, you either work with Bowie or Reed. I also admired John Cale a lot. I was a student living in beautiful Santa Barbara, but I wanted to do something on guitar, if anyone did. So I went to New York, and Lou Reed. I called him when I got there and he gave me a long list of songs to work on. Our first rehearsal was at the old Star Sound. The first song was *Sad Song.* I'd spent 18 hours learning Bob Ezrin's string arrangement. I played it and he watched me with his collar turned up. Afterwards he says softly, 'You're everything you said you were.' Now at last he had a guitarist in his band who could

actually play all the songs off the beloved *Berlin* album he was so panned for. He could incorporate them in his stage show: *Caroline Says, The Kids, Men of Good Fortune, Sad Song.*

To my ears he'd never really had a first-rate guitarist. Hunter and Wagner were decent, sure, but not the same caliber, and Mick Ronson had been very good. Apart from that, they all sucked. Lou himself is a genius guitar player, but with very little technique. He has great ideas, and so he needs someone to translate them. I had all the technique in the world, but not the original ideas. At sound check he'd turn to me: 'How'd you do that? Show me that!' I'd show him, you bend the string, so, before you hit it . . .' Sometimes I knew he was keeping me around as a handy source of information. But I learned so much in the process!

'I rehearsed with Lou through the end of '78 and then in the spring of '79 we went on tour, three weeks at medium venues in Britain and then back to the west coast here. One night in San Francisco we did *Sad Song,* and I realised it was the one night when the band was bad and I was good. Usually the band will be really on – or a couple guys on, a couple off – or we'd *all* be off. But this is the only night I could remember when I alone had a good night. Later I'm relaxing in my hotel room when I get a call from Lou, 'Come up to my room for drinks with me and Sylvia.' She was to become his second wife. I go and he plays me a tape of my solo. Then he plays it over again. 'Chuck,' he said, 'When you took that solo, you levitated the entire room.' The next night, in the dressing room of the Waldorf, he made me a permanent member of the band. 'A permanent member of the band, as long as you don't cross me.' I wanted clarification. He insisted: 'Don't ever lie to me.'

'Next week in Kansas City he came on stage incredibly drunk and banged his guitar against the mike stand. I was the one who had to tune them. He wasn't getting it on. So he pulled the whole band offstage in the middle of a set, the only time he ever did that. He drags everyone into a small room and sits them down. Just us and Sylvia and a roadie or two. He bears down on me with his alcohol breath and screams, 'How could you fuckin' do that to me? I could send you home right now!' He thought it was my fault his guitar was out of tune, after he hit it. Meanwhile outside the whole audience is going crazy. He made me go out there all alone and 're-tune' his guitars. I came back

113

and said, 'Your guitars are now in tune.' Well, we do the show. At the end of the show he takes me aside and says, 'Chuck, you're gonna be very big.'

I was totally and completely his disciple. Not only did I truly love him, but I could play. I feel that only once in the career of any great artist does a qualified disciple come to him because of his work. And I came all the way from Santa Barbara. I feel he hated me because I was so *clean*. When I came out of California, I didn't even drink coffee. I was everything he wasn't, but to reject me was the antithesis of everything he worked for. He was in an emotional trap. For a while it was manageable but he eventually succumbed to the dark side.

"He was completely my hero. When we did the European summer tour of 1979 I remember acts of kindness. I know Lou is supposed to have terrible fights with all his musicians, not to mention managers, but when we toured, I felt he took good care of us. First class everywhere. And finally, when Lou Reed did play *Berlin* in Berlin, at a huge concert hall in the centre of town, I remember walking around with him one afternoon for one of his favourite things, shopping. He was buying tape recorders. We all went out for dinner and I notice Lou is carrying a tape recorder. 'Chuck, I want you to have this.' I was stunned. 'You're a hell of a guitar player.' He'd realised this was my first time on the road, and I hadn't brought along any professional gear for myself.

The biggest nightmare on that tour was when we were playing something like a gymnasium, this was in Germany, that held maybe 2,500 people. American soldiers and German kids. Lou wants it quiet when he's singing *Berlin*.

"Ironically enough, Lou had been lecturing me on showing the proper appreciation and respect for the roadies — 'They can save your life.' But tonight he could not get that audience quiet, and he walked off the stage. Came back. It got noisy again. He left again. He came back in twenty minutes. He saw who was causing the disturbance and he said, 'I want this person ejected.' He had the spotlight brought down. 'Get that person out of here!' From the side, the girl leapt on stage and went for him. He grabbed her and dragged her to the end of the stage, furious, as the road people tried to break them up. Then he lost control and turned and snapped to the band, 'Off the stage'! Lou was so enraged that he grabbed Oley our road manager, a big Swedish guy by the collar and with one hand lifted him off the ground. I didn't

stay around — I knew it wasn't my place.

"Two days later Oley was fired, but he was still with us, crying and begging Lou to let him stay on. Anyway, at that moment we had a riot on our hands. Everyone was throwing chairs and wrecking the stage, and Lou gets arrested! First the German riot police grabbed Oley. They hit the back of his legs with a club. Then they grabbed Lou. Lou remained composed and asked for his leather bag. I was the only one with him — it was one of the few times in my life when I was really terrified. Marty the sax player and Sylvia came in. Lou told them to be cool. Meanwhile we couldn't move. Outside it was like a stampede.

"What does he get charged with? Not inciting to riot, but assaulting this girl! Of course it was all a show. They really wanted to search him and seize drugs so they could claim the capture of Lou Reed, the famous heroin freak! Not a chance — the only hypos I saw the whole tour were the ones some sick fans would toss at the stage. He had nothing, but they made him stay the night.

"There was only one thing that would make Lou Reed cancel a gig automatically: when he assessed that the promoter was cheating him on security. He'd scan an audience of 10,000 and if he didn't see enough security — meaning that he felt he could be hit, or worse — he'd just call off the show. That's why he always played the Bottom Line, in New York, where he could depend upon the security — that was of prime importance.

"Back in London, he also did another kind thing for me. We were playing the Hammersmith Odeon. Lou stopped the set midway and pointed to me and yelled, 'Play!' I took a solo on the Roland Synthesizer. In front of David Bowie, as it turned out, who was standing in the wings. Lou was showing me off — and giving me a real chance for recognition.

"That was the time of the famous Bowie brawl. They had been so close. We were in a restaurant having dinner and Lou asked David to produce *Growing Up in Public*. David said, 'Clean up your act'. He seemed condescending about Lou's work, and maybe his life style too. Lou wasn't on drugs but he was very nervous and under a lot of pressure and he hit him. They yelled at each other and Lou went back to his hotel room. After a short time David stormed over — he wanted to hit Lou back. He was all by himself. Lou made believe he was asleep.

"We finished off the tour that year with five nights at the Bottom Line at Christmas time. I think that was the time we broke the club's record, and it was a fairly happy time for all of us.

"Then in January we went down to the island of Monserrat to record *Growing Up in Public.* There were many things wrong with this album. Personally, I don't think Lou was sure he wanted a hit record out of Arista; he wanted to do some thing quiet and meaningful. He was caught, again, between being Lou Reed and being successful. But he did come out with some beautiful pieces — *Teach the Gifted Children* especially was fantastic. Others — I think he leaned on Michael Fonfara too much. But it was only a few weeks before his marriage to Sylvia, and his mind was involved with that.

"Historically, this album is very important. It's the first full use of the guitar synthesizer — except for *The Bells,* where Lou played on some songs. One night we were all down at the only restaurant on the island with Sylvia. Lou came over and put his arm around me. He said, 'There are only two other musicians in this world with talent like yours, Don Cherry and John Cale.' At that point I felt we had a very strong bond.

"Well, the album was not well received. And Arista did *not* promote it — this is after that fight at the Bottom Line, where Lou yelled at Clive from the stage, 'I need money to live!' Right in the middle of *Men of Good Fortune.* Maybe Clive felt this didn't have what it took, either. Maybe we didn't work hard enough on it. We were down there three weeks to the day — and Lou did do all the vocals in one take. But he had fulfilled his contract with Arista — I believe it was for four records — even though he was unhappy about their poor support.

"In April, after we'd been back a few weeks, I got a call from David Bowie's assistant, Coco. 'David would really like you to lay some tracks on his new record.' Great! *Ashes to Ashes* became a big hit in England and Europe. Directly afterwards I got a call from Lou. Of course I told him everything. I was only totally honest with the man. 'And — of course — he paid you?' 'Yes — triple scale.' Of course it was Lou who exposed me to David in the first place — I knew that. And then I did some tracks for Garland Jeffreys' *Escape Artist.*

"That summer we did our most wildly successful tour — he really made money. In our European tour the summer before, he had carefully played a whole lot of medium venues, working very hard and staying away from the capital cities. This summer he made the real killing; 60,000 seats, instead of 3,000. Sometimes a 80,000 people would show up — think of that! We were driven to and from the stadium in police cars. It had been a brilliant strategy on Lou's part, but that's when the crunch started to come down with his band. I myself felt he was very fair with us but Michael Suchorsky, for instance, who had been with him five years, wasn't that thrilled with European touring. Michael wanted his own room but as there were five of us in the group, we alternated room assignments. He felt resentful because we were playing before so many thousands of people, and he was still living in a small apartment on the Lower East Side — he was very discouraged by the setup. I felt I was working with the best band in New York, touring Europe, and being paid more than fairly — why louse it up? Room arrangments and playing longer didn't matter to me. But some members would see all those people ... there was maybe something to that. If he'd have given the band the proceeds from just one concert, we could each have done something on our own back in New York. But we were only salaried. There are things to say on both sides — *he* had worked very hard to get to this point.

"Anyway, the damage was done. When we got back to the US, we went out to the coast in the fall and did Don Kirshner and played some dates in California. Lou was getting more and more annoyed — he has a very short tolerance for other people's complaints. Maybe he also felt guilty about having all that money in his pocket and finding reasons why no one else should have it. By the time we got back here, to go into the studio and put down some tracks for an animation film (with MGM), he started to pull away. This one was always asking for more money, this one was always getting stoned, this one was eating constantly and always asking if we could order in. My personal obsession was becoming a guitar hero, but Lou could go along with that. At least, that's what I felt at the time.

"There was a fight during the studio recording about overtime — a few hundred dollars. Lou was furious. I think that was the final straw. He couldn't see that we all were struggling. He felt that with our experience, we should simply build on it and go out and earn more on our own. That's what I tried to do.

"Nobody actually knew they were fired. They just did the animation tracks — and that was it. We were aware that Lou was very unhappy,

Sylvia Morales 1977 *Godlis*

and he once called someone a jerk.

"I knew that if I was going to maintain a relationship with this man, I'd have to be very vanilla with him. Now at this time I was flirting heavily with RCA for a solo record deal. My understanding was that Lou had some sort of production obligation with them — he could produce any artist he chose. The label seemed very much in favour of our working together. We worked on the music every morning — he lived around the block, and we'd walk his dachshunds, and he'd tell me how mad he was at this one or that one in the band. I could sense he was looking for something to get *me* on. I really hoped I didn't mess it up, I had such a dream of working with him. Whatever wrangling went down, when it comes to his music, I love him. He had introduced me to the Roland Guitar Synthesizer and encouraged me, complimented me in front of others. We'd spent two years on the road together and had some incredibly close moments. And now we were going to make this killer guitar album together.

"I worked very hard to get a solo deal with RCA and by the late autumn, I had it. I was working with Lou almost every morning. Sylvia would be at school and he'd call and say, 'Come on over and bring your guitar.' I felt very confident, very optimistic. But then came the hideous head games. Everyone I wanted in the studio with me, Lou wanted fired. These people were qualified, close friends who'd been with me from the start, but Lou wanted complete control. He always had what looked like good reasons, but I couldn't take it. Finally, he had his manager call and tell me to fire my last ally, Charlie, who did all my demos. I wanted one friend at my side. I refused. I needed one frame of reference! How can you make an album with no ego?

"Lou said something like he'd have to go and tell the label that the artist was uncooperative. I couldn't believe this. I had worked so hard. I didn't talk to him for five days and finally I was so mad I called and told him he didn't give a damn about me or my work. 'Where is the artist that made *Berlin*?' I said. He told me to call back when I had something to say.

"The deal dissolved. The A&R man who had signed me went on to a different job. Even though Lou was officially slated to produce me, it never happened. He shot the whole thing out from under me by making me choose between what I believed was right . . . and Lou Reed. The last time we saw each other was by accident in the neighbourhood. We shared a taxi uptown and discussed things. Somehow, he got me to admit I'd make a 'mistake'. Maybe I did make the wrong choice, commercially.

"We had such a history. I could never look back on that with anything but happiness, even awe. The dream I brought with me from Santa Barbara was ten times larger in real life. We worked so well together, and he gave me so much. I gave him everything I had, everything I could think to give. I don't really think he'll get another musician with the same emotional impact I brought to that group . . . the devoted disciple.

"A few months afterwards, I picked up a small book of his songs in a music store. I looked at his picture; it all came flooding back. I knew I could never walk around for the rest of my life pretending to hate Lou Reed. I called him up.

"I said, 'I just wanted to tell you that I really loved you.'

"Lou paused only a moment. He said, 'I can appreciate that.'"

Lou Reed and Sylvia Morales were married in his Greenwich Village loft on Valentine's Day, 1980, by New York State Supreme Court Justice Ernest Rosenberger. The joyful affair included their families, Lou's about-to-be-ex band, his college chum Garland Jeffreys, Susan Springfield, his manager, Eric Kronfeld, a very few media intimates and RCA Records President Bob Summer and his wife. Clive Davis, conspicuous by his absence, was at an Arista sales convention in L.A. The short vows were written by Lou from two poems by Delmore Schwartz. Sylvia, 24, wore her mother's satin and tulle wedding dress, with gardenias in her hair. Lou, looking 19 according to some of those present, wore a suit and tie and was deliriously happy. After the ceremony, everyone toasted the couple then went off to a nearby restaurant for wedding cake and champagne. Then Lou and Sylvia changed into less formal attire — including, in Lou's case, a leather jacket — and everyone piled into limos and sped off to Playland on Times Square where the celebrants played pinball till the cows came home.

Lou with Debbie Harry of Blondie and Iggy Pop *Ebet Roberts*

THE BLUE MASK

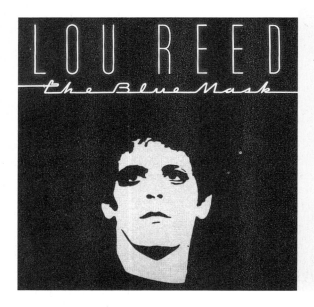

"My goal is to make an album that would speak to people the way Joyce speaks to me."
Lou Reed

Lou Reed's sixteenth solo album is nothing less than his resurrection into the fullness of life. More than an affirmation of faith, it is the triumph of an artist who risked everything, again, for "the glory of love". It is a paeon to his wife Sylvia, to his mentor Delmore Schwartz, to the musician himself and to the fans who have loved him, in varying degrees, for seventeen years. It is the final repudiation of a career full of ricocheting cheap shots, to those who would insist the shots defined the man: the peroxided parodies, the tying off with microphone cords, the lurches offstage, the brawls with critics, the franchised lawsuits, the sets that, some felt, delivered short. *The Blue Mask* is a beautiful, brilliant moving testament to "the terrible beauty he's borne", in the words of Robert Christgau.

The album is divided between the domestic delights of a rock and roll animal comfy in his suburban Jersey lair and the voyeur/raconteur who reports with clarity on the evil around him. If the four albums of the Velvet Underground were a progression to adaptation to the modern world, *The Blue Mask*, released in early February of 1982, seemed to carry the message that the horror will not go away and the only hope of salvation is to work for the love of another.

"There's this real myth, as if by getting married you suddenly become old and senile and move to the suburbs and never do a meaningful piece of work again. I envision marriage as the great romantic thing it is. How can you write about love when you don't believe in it?" he recently told Steve Dupler in *International Musician*. In forging an authentic "Easter" album he has transcended — not without calculation — the traps of his literary peers and inspirations. He does not drink himself to death in front of a TV set in Lowell, Massachusetts, as Kerouac; he does not suffer the despair and self-annihilation of John Berryman; he is not brought down by spiritual loss and physical abuse, as Schwartz. He not only endures, but he prevails, turning the imbalances of the last decade — not for nothing is the album cover modelled after *Transformer*, his first commercial success — into fine art.

"The worst thing that happened was that occasionally he was impatient at not getting the recognition he thought he deserved. But now he is a master showman; to me, he's like Maurice Chevalier, and can go on forever."

. . . and even going on forever on RCA Records, to which he returned after oft-proclaimed unhappiness with Arista. If longevity at a label, especially one so beleaguered with lawsuits and counter-accusations, is any mark of real stardom, their decade together goes far beyond the schemes of commerce. Indeed *The Blue Mask*, though championed by the critics, had rather limited sales and made it to #169 on the Billboard (US) charts in early March — roughly the exact niche of *The Velvet Underground & Nico*. Some considered that his refusal to tour at all contributed to this. "I've never been straight on stage," the artist told Lisa Robinson, finding it a much wiser course to work out his artistic obsessions in the studio. "Maybe one night at the Bottom Line," he said to Steve Dupler. "But as far as 90 days/89 cities — I can't do that anymore."

His refusal to maintain the image of the onstage monster, screaming on pharmaceuticals, irritated some, but the terrible personal cost is not a consideration to the Lou Reed fan waiting for *his* man. "He's banished himself to the suburbs of his imagination . . . a lazy, undignified disgrace," snapped Mark Cordery in *New Musical Express*.

The stark, declamatory poetry of the album is supported by a trio of handpicked New York musicians, Fernando Saunders on fretless

Steve Katz

124

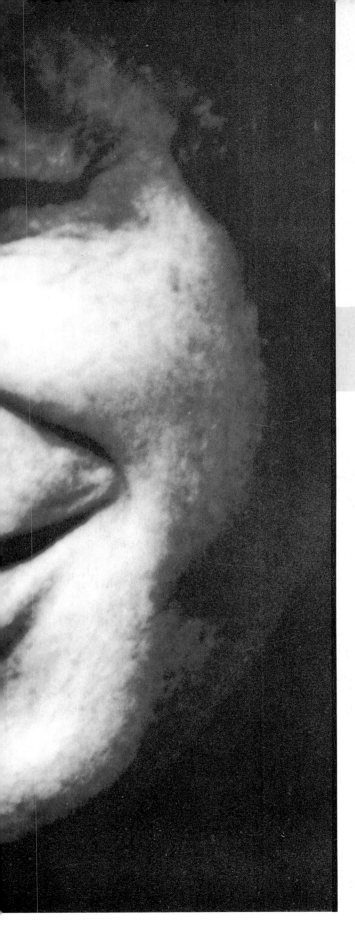

bass, Doane Perry on drums and the underground legend Robert Quine on guitar. Quine, a master of powerful understatement, interacts with Lou's guitar lines to produce a well constructed, emotionally devastating whole. "If Delmore Schwartz" (to whom the work is dedicated) "is at the spiritual centre of the record," wrote Brian Cullman, "Quine is clearly at the musical centre."

Cullman echoes the feelings of many Reed supporters when he states that it's the record "I'd given up all hope of Lou Reed ever making, musically, emotionally and spiritually." Robert Palmer in *The New York Times* termed it "the most powerful and the most consistent album (he) has made since his 1967 recording debut with the Velvet Underground — and he knows it." Lou tells him, in an rare interview, "It's mostly working with the right musicians." He dissolved his former band, some of whose members had been with him over five years, when he realised his own sound seemed "isolated", and there was "a certain confidence that's not there because (I wasn't) really in control." He is totally in control of every note of *The Blue Mask*, which seems the emotional successor to the song *Street Hassle* and the resolution of the interpersonal anguish explored most acutely in *Berlin*. In terms of its passionate but disciplined love of language, it relates most directly to his two masterworks, *Street Hassle* and *Heroin*. With *The Blue Mask*, Delmore can indeed sleep in peace (although Lou tells us he walks about upstairs with ghostly footsteps); his disciple has kept the faith.

Now forty, self-assured, solvent, and able to purge from his space the two hazards to his emotional health, touring and those who make their living via the typewriter, this brilliant American artist can indeed go on forever. He has had the balls to go out and get precisely what he needs, at hideous personal expense; the result is not arrogance, but a progressive enlightenment we are privileged to share. The new Lou Reed seems to say, "there are problems in this time/And all of them are mine" . . . musically, at least. If risk is the only antidote to reality, he is only to be admired for throwing himself out there and making the leap we see vicariously, from the safety of far away.

DISCOGRAPHY

THE VELVET UNDERGROUND
THE VELVET UNDERGROUND & NICO
MGM/Verve 5008 (UK) Verve 2315-056

WHITE LIGHT/WHITE HEAT
MGM/Verve 5046 (UK) Verve 2353-024

THE VELVET UNDERGROUND (third album)
MGM/Verve 2353 022

LOADED
Atlantic/Cotillion SD 9034

THE VELVET UNDERGROUND LIVE AT MAX'S KANSAS CITY
Atlantic/Cotillion SD 9500

SQUEEZE
Atlantic (UK)

1969 VELVET UNDERGROUND LIVE
Mercury/Phonogram SRM-2-7504

ARCHETYPES (White LIght/White Heat)
MGM M3F 4950 1974

ANDY WARHOL'S VELVET UNDERGROUND FEATURING NICO
MGM 2683 006 (UK)

LOU REED AND THE VELVET UNDERGROUND
MGM Pride 0022 1973

THE STORY OF THE VELVET UNDERGROUND
Polydor 2664 405 Germany

VELVET UNDERGROUND
MGM 2354 033 (UK)

VELVET UNDERGROUND
MGM GAS-131

LOU REED

LOU REED (first solo)
RCA LSP-4701

TRANSFORMER
RCA AFLI-4807

BERLIN
RCA INTS 5150

ROCK N ROLL ANIMAL
RCA AFLI – 0472

SALLY CAN'T DANCE
RCA CPLI – 0611

LOU REED LIVE
RCA APLI – 0959

METAL MACHINE MUSIC
RCA CPL2 – 1101

CONEY ISLAND BABY
RCA ANLI – 2480

ROCK AND ROLL HEART
Arista 4100

STREET HASSLE
Arista 4169

TAKE NO PRISONERS/LIVE
Arista 8502

THE BELLS
Arista AB 4229